Preface

Welcome to "100 Business Ideas," a guidebook designed to inspire and empower aspiring entrepreneurs like you. In these pages, you will find a curated collection of innovative business concepts spanning various industries and sectors. Whether you're a seasoned entrepreneur looking for your next venture or someone dreaming of starting their first business, this book aims to spark creativity, provide valuable insights, and guide you towards potential opportunities in the dynamic world of business.

Starting a business is more than just a financial endeavor; it's a journey of passion, resilience, and strategic thinking. Each idea presented here has been carefully selected for its potential to meet current market demands, leverage emerging trends, or address specific niche markets. Whether you're interested in technology and innovation, retail and e-commerce, services and consulting, or any other sector, you'll find a diverse range of ideas to explore and consider.

Throughout these pages, you'll discover practical tips on validating your business ideas, understanding market dynamics, and taking the first steps towards launching your venture. Remember, entrepreneurship is about embracing challenges, learning from failures, and constantly adapting to changes in the business landscape.

As you embark on this journey of exploration and discovery, we encourage you to approach each idea with an open mind and a readiness to innovate. The future of business belongs to those who dare to dream, take calculated risks, and turn their visions into reality.

Let "100 Business Ideas" be your companion in this exciting venture. May it inspire you, ignite your entrepreneurial spirit, and guide you towards building a successful and impactful business.

Note from the Author

I have papers filled with ideas, research, Q/As, future plans for hundreds of business ideas that I have wanted to pursue like my only passion at some point of my life. Thing is for each of these ideas, when I was working on planning my business around that idea, my life was revolving around it. Awake, asleep, conversations, thoughts, everything at that point of my life revolved around that particular idea. Be it starting a consulting firm, building an app, leverage technology to build services like digital events catering and management or starting an education platform, whatever idea I was working on, my whole life before that made sense to me at that time, it all aligned to that idea and I could imagine the change I would bring with this business into people's lives and my own. That particular idea and its planning felt to be my truth at that point of time.

But another inevitable truth I realise today, was that I found one 'practical' reason or another to give up on each of these ideas at some point of time. Either it wasn't meant for the market I was in or I 'couldn't' manage to arrange for the human/financial resources to start the business. There were times I didn't have enough 'courage', or had other 'priorities'. Whatever it maybe, there was something. Something that seemed more important at that point of time, or 'easier' and 'achievable', or let's use the most appropriate word- 'Known'.

To summarise, I couldn't navigate from Planning phase of any of my businesses to Execution. I see planning as period when you imagine or manifest a new future, different from the current or expected future in the manner that your business and everything related to it exists in that future you are planning. Execution phase to me is jumping into that imagination and the 'Unknown' where what you planned will or will not happen. Once you jump into it, you need to be ready for both scenarios. Probability is you might have to change your initial plan uncountable times to reach your destination or Pilot launch your business idea. Everyday, every person you meet can bring a new challenge, a new unimagined question, another unknown reason for you to give up, and all that will make sense to you, sound 'practical' to you. And latter will be a consistent state for the initial months at least. Question is - What do you believe in?

If you have decided to become an entrepreneur, there is only one practical thing to do- the one you convince your mind to believe in and practice everyday, every moment till you finally achieve your goal. People's best or worst advices, are only based on their own life experiences and if you have imagined a life and future they haven't lived, then I would just suggest to believe in the unknown you have imagined for yourself and not the known others have existed in. Every time you have 100 reasons to give up, are you able to find 101 to keep going?

Every reason you convince your mind why you can't today- Maybe ask one more time if that will be a good enough reason for your future self justifying why you 'couldn't'.

I was raised in a family of 5, my parents, who gave me all they could, they still do, and my siblings- a younger sister and a brother, who brightened up my life everyday just by being around as my best admirers and critics. They have eaten the worst and best of my recipes, and have heard intently and profoundly to my best and worst business ideas too. My father has believed in me like no one else. He looks up to me as the most successful person, someone who can achieve anything in life. That thought has given me the sky to imagine and pursue anything. My mother, she is the strongest person I have known all my life. And thing is I realise that only today. Since I remember, she is the most soft-spoken, kind-hearted and giving person I have ever seen. I have seen her living every moment for her kids. Only for her, I am able to believe today, that kind can be strong, in fact, stronger than everyone and everything else. Mumma, I owe this life to you. My family has been in different businesses for years and that probably served to my entrepreneurial interests. As a B.Tech student, after college hours, I would make time for extra endeavours and planning. It would sometimes be teaching school kids, soft skills training classes, or exploring technology markets and opportunities.

Right after my college, I started a digital marketing company, that kept going for some time, I didn't put efforts to scale it and was always exploring other opportunities. I remember dreaming of being listed in Forbes 30 Under 30 with a big business idea one day. I would sit late nights, analyse the world around me, jot down all my ideas and pickup one that clicked. Next few weeks, months and for some of them, just days will be exploring its potential and feasibility.

After all these years, when I got my hands on my work, it seemed so precious. This time, I couldn't let go of the value and potential they hold. While it won't be plausible to execute a hundred business ideas, it is definitely possible to share them with hundreds of people who could pick their big business idea or maybe just gather some inspiration to pursue what they have already thought of.

Ergo, this book for You!

My Best Wishes to the Reader!
I hope you find what you desire!

Gazal

INDEX

1. Introduction
   - Why Start a Business?
   - How to Use This Book

2. Tech and Innovation
   - Idea 1: AI-Powered Customer Service Solutions
   - Idea 2: Virtual Reality Training Programs
   - Idea 3: Block chain for Supply Chain Management
   - Idea 4: Drone Delivery Services
   - Idea 5: Smart Home Device Installation Services
   - Idea 6: Augmented Reality Gaming Applications
   - Idea 7: Cyber security Consulting Firm
   - Idea 8: Mobile App Development Agency
   - Idea 9: Internet of Things (IoT) Solutions Provider
   - Idea 10: Biometric Security Systems
   - Idea 11: Data Analytics and Business Intelligence Services
   - Idea 12: Cloud Computing Solutions

3. Retail and E-Commerce
   - Idea 13: Subscription Box Services
   - Idea 14: Online Marketplace for Local Artisans
   - Idea 15: Eco-Friendly Fashion Brand
   - Idea 16: Personalized Gift Services
   - Idea 17: Customized Meal Kit Delivery
   - Idea 18: Vintage and Retro Clothing Store
   - Idea 19: Online Bookstore for Rare and Collectible Books
   - Idea 20: Organic and Natural Beauty Products E-commerce Platform
   - Idea 21: Specialty Tea and Coffee Subscription Service
   - Idea 22: Customized Furniture Design and Sales Platform

4. Services and Consulting
   - Idea 23: Virtual Personal Assistant Services
   - Idea 24: Business Efficiency Consulting
   - Idea 25: Sustainable Event Planning
   - Idea 26: Freelance Writing and Editing Services
   - Idea 27: Career Coaching and Resume Writing
   - Idea 28: Digital Marketing Agency
   - Idea 29: Social Media Management Consulting
   - Idea 30: Human Resources Outsourcing Services
   - Idea 31: Market Research and Analysis Firm

- Idea 32: Legal Consulting for Startups and Small Businesses
- Idea 33: Strategic Planning and Advisory Services
- Idea 34: IT Support and Managed Services

5. Health and Wellness
   - Idea 35: Personalized Nutrition Counseling
   - Idea 36: Mental Health and Wellness Apps
   - Idea 37: Fitness Subscription Boxes
   - Idea 38: Telemedicine Services
   - Idea 39: Mobile Fitness Training
   - Idea 40: Meditation and Mindfulness Classes

6. Food and Beverage
   - Idea 41: Plant-Based Fast Food Chain
   - Idea 42: Specialty Coffee Roastery
   - Idea 43: Craft Beer Subscription Service
   - Idea 44: Food Truck Business
   - Idea 45: Gourmet Popcorn Shop
   - Idea 46: Artisanal Ice Cream Production

7. Finance and Investment
   - Idea 47: Peer-to-Peer Lending Platform
   - Idea 48: Financial Literacy Courses for Teens
   - Idea 49: Impact Investing Fund
   - Idea 50: Robo-Advisory Services
   - Idea 51: Cryptocurrency Investment Advisory
   - Idea 52: Tax Preparation and Advisory Services

8. Education and Training
   - Idea 53: Online Language Learning Platform
   - Idea 54: Coding Boot camps for Kids
   - Idea 55: Virtual Reality Educational Experiences
   - Idea 56: Online Tutoring Services
   - Idea 57: Music Lessons and Instrument Rentals
   - Idea 58: Career Skills Development Workshops

9. Sustainability and Green Business
   - Idea 59: Urban Farming Solutions
   - Idea 60: Renewable Energy Consultancy
   - Idea 61: Eco-Friendly Packaging Solutions
   - Idea 62: Upcycled Furniture Design
   - Idea 63: Water Purification Systems
   - Idea 64: Sustainable Fashion Rental Service

10. Creative Arts and Media
   - Idea 65: Digital Content Creation Agency
   - Idea 66: Online Art Classes
   - Idea 67: Podcast Production Studio
   - Idea 68: Video Production Services
   - Idea 69: Graphic Design and Branding Agency
   - Idea 70: Photography Studio

11. Real Estate and Property
   - Idea 71: Property Management Services
   - Idea 72: Vacation Rental Management
   - Idea 73: Sustainable Architecture Firm
   - Idea 74: Real Estate Investment Trust (REIT)
   - Idea 75: Home Staging Services
   - Idea 76: Property Inspection Services

12. Manufacturing and Production
   - Idea 77: 3D Printing Services
   - Idea 78: Custom Furniture Design
   - Idea 79: Biodegradable Product Manufacturing
   - Idea 80: Organic Skincare Product Line
   - Idea 81: Specialty Chemical Manufacturing
   - Idea 82: Customized Jewelry Design

13. Tourism and Hospitality
   - Idea 83: Cultural Tours and Experiences
   - Idea 84: Boutique Hotel Chain
   - Idea 85: Adventure Travel Agency
   - Idea 86: Eco-Tourism Packages
   - Idea 87: Local Food and Wine Tours
   - Idea 88: Luxury Yacht Charter Services

14. Social Impact and Nonprofit
   - Idea 89: Community Kitchen and Food Distribution
   - Idea 90: Mobile Health Clinics
   - Idea 91: Youth Mentorship Program
   - Idea 92: Environmental Conservation Nonprofit
   - Idea 93: Refugee Support Services
   - Idea 94: Animal Rescue and Adoption Center

15. Miscellaneous
   - Idea 95: Pet Care and Grooming Services

- Idea 96: Subscription Service for Seniors
- Idea 97: Event Planning and Coordination
- Idea 98: Car Rental and Ride-Sharing Service
- Idea 99: Language Translation Services
- Idea 100: Vintage Car Restoration

16. Conclusion
    - Next Steps
    - Final Thoughts

Introduction

Why Start a Business

Starting a business offers you the opportunity to transform your ideas into tangible solutions, contribute to the economy, and create value for your customers and communities. It's a chance to carve your own path, pursue your passions, and make a meaningful impact on the world around you.

How to Use This Book

This book is structured to help you explore a wide range of business ideas systematically. Here's how you can make the most of "100 Business Ideas":

- Explore Diverse Industries: Dive into various sectors such as technology, retail, services, finance, education, and more. Each section provides insights into different industries to broaden your perspective.
- Discover Innovative Concepts: Discover detailed descriptions of each business idea, including market opportunities, potential challenges, and scalability considerations.
- Evaluate Market Potential: Use the market insights provided to assess the viability of each business idea in your target market. Consider factors such as customer demographics, competition analysis, and market trends.
- Validate Your Ideas: Utilize the validation tips and exercises to assess the feasibility and profitability of your chosen business ideas. Validate assumptions, conduct market research, and refine your concepts based on real-world data.
- Develop Your Business Plan: Use the structured approach to develop a comprehensive business plan for your chosen idea. Outline your vision, mission, target audience, marketing strategy, operational plan, and financial projections.
- Navigate Startup Challenges: Gain practical advice on overcoming common startup challenges such as funding, legal considerations, team building, and initial marketing efforts.
- Inspiration and Adaptation: While each idea is presented as a starting point, feel free to adapt and innovate based on your unique skills, experiences, and market insights.

Introduction to Tech and Innovation Businesses

Welcome to the Tech and Innovation section of "100 Business Ideas." This section explores cutting-edge technologies and innovative business models that are reshaping industries and creating new opportunities for entrepreneurs. From artificial intelligence and block chain to virtual reality and IoT solutions, these ideas harness the power of technology to address current market needs, enhance efficiency, and drive future growth. Whether you're passionate about developing groundbreaking software solutions, exploring the potential of emerging technologies, or revolutionizing traditional industries, this section offers a range of exciting ventures to inspire and guide your entrepreneurial journey.

1. AI-Powered Customer Service Solutions

Description: Develop artificial intelligence-based platforms to enhance customer service interactions, automate responses, and provide personalized customer support experiences.

Marketing Insights and Opportunities:
- Growing Demand: Businesses are increasingly adopting AI to improve customer service efficiency and customer satisfaction.
- Target Industries: Focus on sectors such as e-commerce, telecommunications, and financial services where customer interaction volumes are high.
- Personalization: Highlight how AI can customize responses based on customer behavior and preferences, improving engagement.

Requirements to Start:
- AI Expertise: Access to AI developers and data scientists to build and maintain the AI algorithms or just leverage existing AI tools and technologies to create your service.
- Data Integration: Ability to integrate with existing CRM systems and customer data platforms.
- Compliance: Ensure compliance with data protection regulations (e.g., GDPR, CCPA) when handling customer data.

Challenges:
- Algorithm Accuracy: Ensuring AI accurately understands and responds to customer queries.
- Customer Acceptance: Overcoming potential resistance or skepticism towards AI-powered interactions.
- Cost of Implementation: Initial investment in AI technology and ongoing maintenance costs can be substantial.

Scalability Opportunities:

- Expansion to New Markets: Scale across different industries beyond initial target sectors.
- Feature Enhancement: Offer additional AI functionalities like sentiment analysis or predictive analytics.
- Partnerships: Collaborate with CRM providers or industry-specific platforms to expand reach and capabilities.

Roadmap:
1. Research and Development: Develop robust AI algorithms and test with pilot customers.
2. Launch and Iterate: Deploy initial version, gather feedback, and iterate based on user interactions.
3. Scaling Operations: Expand customer base while refining AI capabilities for scalability.
4. Partnership and Integration: Collaborate with CRM providers for seamless integration and enhanced features.

Further Resources:
- AI and Customer Service: A Practical Guide by Harvard Business Review
- AI Trends and Innovations: Insights from Gartner Research

2. Virtual Reality Training Programs

Description: Create immersive virtual reality (VR) experiences for training purposes, such as simulations for healthcare procedures, industrial safety protocols, or employee skill development.

Marketing Insights and Opportunities:
- Training Efficiency: VR offers realistic training scenarios that enhance learning outcomes compared to traditional methods.
- Industry Applications: Target sectors like healthcare, manufacturing, and education where hands-on training is critical.
- Customization: Provide tailored VR solutions that meet specific training needs of organizations, ensuring higher engagement.

Requirements to Start:
- VR Development Expertise: Access to VR developers and content creators skilled in creating immersive experiences.
- Hardware Compatibility: Ensure compatibility with VR headsets and equipment used by target industries.
- Content Licensing: Obtain necessary licenses for using proprietary training materials or simulations.

Challenges:
- High Initial Investment: Cost of VR equipment and software development can be prohibitive for some organizations.
- Content Quality: Ensuring high-quality, realistic simulations that effectively convey learning objectives.

- User Adaptation: Addressing potential discomfort or motion sickness issues experienced by some VR users.

Scalability Opportunities:
- Industry Expansion: Extend VR training programs to new industries beyond initial target sectors.
- Advanced Features: Integrate AI for personalized learning paths or real-time performance feedback.
- Global Reach: Offer remote training solutions that transcend geographical limitations through cloud-based VR platforms.

Roadmap:
1. Needs Assessment: Identify specific training needs and objectives of target industries through consultations.
2. Content Development: Create VR simulations in collaboration with subject matter experts and instructional designers.
3. Pilot Testing: Conduct trials with early adopters to gather feedback and refine content.
4. Deployment and Support: Roll out VR training programs with ongoing technical support and content updates.

Further Resources:
- VR Training Solutions: Best Practices and Case Studies
- VR in Education and Workforce Development: Insights from Industry Leaders

3. Block chain for Supply Chain Management

Description: Implement block chain technology to enhance transparency, traceability, and efficiency in supply chain operations, ensuring secure transactions and reducing fraud.

Marketing Insights and Opportunities:
- Supply Chain Transparency: Address growing consumer demand for ethical sourcing and sustainability through block chain-enabled transparency.
- Regulatory Compliance: Offer solutions that facilitate compliance with global trade regulations and standards.
- Cost Savings: Highlight potential cost reductions in logistics and inventory management through streamlined processes.

Requirements to Start:
- Block chain Development Expertise: Access to block chain developers skilled in creating decentralized ledger systems.
- Industry Partnerships: Collaborate with logistics providers, manufacturers, and retailers to integrate block chain solutions.
- Data Security: Implement robust encryption and authentication mechanisms to protect sensitive supply chain data.

Challenges:

- Industry Adoption: Convincing traditional supply chain stakeholders of the benefits and security of block chain technology.
- Integration Complexity: Overcoming interoperability issues when integrating block chain with existing ERP and inventory systems.
- Scalability: Ensuring block chain networks can handle large-scale supply chain operations without compromising performance.

Scalability Opportunities:
- Cross-Border Trade: Expand block chain solutions to facilitate international trade and cross-border transactions.
- Smart Contracts: Implement smart contracts for automated payment processing and contract enforcement.
- Data Analytics: Leverage block chain data for predictive analytics and supply chain optimization.

Roadmap:
1. Pilot Projects: Launch pilot projects with select partners to demonstrate block chain benefits and gather real-world data.
2. Network Expansion: Scale block chain solutions across supply chain nodes, involving key stakeholders in each phase.
3. Regulatory Compliance: Ensure compliance with data protection laws and industry standards throughout implementation.
4. Continuous Improvement: Iterate based on feedback and technological advancements to enhance block chain capabilities.

Further Resources:
- Block chain in Supply Chain: Implementation Guide
- Case Studies on Block chain Adoption in Logistics and Manufacturing

4. IoT Solutions for Smart Home Automation

Description: Develop Internet of Things (IoT) solutions that enable homeowners to automate and control devices such as lighting, security systems, and appliances through mobile apps or voice commands.

Marketing Insights and Opportunities:
- Growing Market: Increasing adoption of smart home devices due to convenience and energy efficiency benefits.
- Target Audience: Appeal to tech-savvy homeowners and property developers interested in integrating IoT into residential properties.
- Integration with AI: Combine IoT with AI for predictive maintenance and personalized home automation experiences.

Requirements to Start:
- IoT Hardware Expertise: Partner with hardware manufacturers or develop proprietary IoT devices and sensors.
- Mobile App Development: Create user-friendly apps for remote monitoring and control of IoT devices.

- Data Security: Implement encryption protocols and secure cloud storage for user data protection.

Challenges:
- Interoperability: Ensuring compatibility among different IoT devices and platforms.
- Privacy Concerns: Addressing consumer apprehensions about data privacy and cyber security risks.
- Market Fragmentation: Navigating a fragmented market with various standards and protocols for IoT devices.

Scalability Opportunities:
- Expansion to Commercial Properties: Scale IoT solutions for office buildings, hotels, and retail spaces.
- Energy Management: Offer energy monitoring and optimization services to reduce utility costs for homeowners and businesses.
- Partnerships: Collaborate with real estate developers and home builders to integrate IoT as a standard feature in new construction projects.

Roadmap:
1. Product Development: Design and prototype IoT devices and companion apps.
2. Testing and Certification: Conduct rigorous testing for reliability, security, and compatibility.
3. Market Launch: Roll out products with targeted marketing campaigns and user feedback collection.
4. Customer Support: Provide ongoing support and updates to enhance product functionality and user experience.

Further Resources:
- IoT Trends and Innovations: Insights from Industry Experts
- Smart Home Automation: Best Practices and Implementation Strategies

5. Augmented Reality for Retail Experiences

Description: Create augmented reality (AR) applications that enhance retail experiences by allowing customers to visualize products in their environment before making purchase decisions.

Marketing Insights and Opportunities:
- Enhanced Shopping Experience: AR enhances engagement by offering interactive product demos and virtual try-on.
- Retail Integration: Partner with retail chains and e-commerce platforms to integrate AR into their shopping apps.
- Branding and Marketing: Use AR to create memorable brand experiences and drive customer loyalty.

Requirements to Start:
- AR Development Expertise: Access to AR developers and 3D artists skilled in creating immersive retail experiences.

- Content Creation: Develop high-quality 3D models and animations of products for AR visualization.
- Hardware Compatibility: Ensure compatibility with AR-enabled smart phones and devices.

Challenges:
- User Adoption: Educating consumers about AR technology and its benefits in the retail context.
- Technical Limitations: Addressing potential latency issues and ensuring smooth AR experiences.
- Content Maintenance: Regularly updating AR content to reflect product changes and seasonal promotions.

Scalability Opportunities:
- Cross-Sector Integration: Expand AR applications beyond retail to industries such as real estate and tourism.
- Social Commerce: Integrate social sharing features within AR experiences to encourage user-generated content and viral marketing.
- Data Analytics: Analyze user interaction data to optimize AR features and personalize shopping recommendations.

Roadmap:
1. Concept Development: Define AR features and functionalities that align with retail partner needs.
2. Prototyping and Testing: Build prototypes and conduct usability tests to refine AR application performance.
3. Deployment Strategy: Partner with retail brands for phased rollouts across stores and online platforms.
4. Marketing and Promotion: Launch marketing campaigns to drive awareness and adoption among target consumers.

Further Resources:
- Augmented Reality in Retail: Strategies for Success
- AR Development Tools and Platforms: Comparative Analysis

6. AI-Powered Personal Finance Management

Description: Develop AI-driven applications that provide personalized financial advice, budgeting tools, and investment recommendations to individuals.

Marketing Insights and Opportunities:
- Financial Wellness: Address increasing consumer interest in managing personal finances effectively and achieving financial goals.
- Target Demographics: Appeal to millennials and Gen Z consumers accustomed to digital banking and fintech solutions.
- Data Security: Highlight robust encryption and data privacy measures to build trust with users.

Requirements to Start:

- AI and Machine Learning Expertise: Access to data scientists and AI engineers proficient in financial modeling and algorithm development.
- Data Aggregation: Integrate with financial institutions' APIs to access user transaction data securely.
- Regulatory Compliance: Ensure compliance with financial regulations and data protection laws.

Challenges:
- Algorithm Accuracy: Developing AI models that provide accurate financial advice tailored to individual user profiles.
- Customer Trust: Overcoming skepticism about AI's ability to handle sensitive financial information.
- Market Competition: Competing with established financial management apps and digital banking solutions.

Scalability Opportunities:
- Subscription Models: Offer premium features or subscription plans for advanced financial insights and portfolio management.
- Partnerships: Collaborate with banks, fintech startups, or employers to offer AI-powered financial wellness programs.
- Global Expansion: Scale services internationally by adapting to local financial regulations and consumer behaviors.

Roadmap:
1. Prototype Development: Build MVP (Minimum Viable Product) with core financial management features.
2. User Feedback: Gather feedback from early adopters to iterate and enhance AI algorithms.
3. Monetization Strategy: Define pricing models and value-added services to generate revenue.
4. Customer Acquisition: Implement marketing strategies to acquire and retain users through targeted campaigns and referrals.

Further Resources:
- AI in Finance: Applications and Case Studies
- Personal Finance Management Apps: Comparative Analysis and Market Trends

7. Drone Delivery Services

Description: Develop drone delivery solutions for transporting goods and packages over short to medium distances, providing faster and more efficient logistics solutions.

Marketing Insights and Opportunities:
- Logistics Efficiency: Drones offer expedited delivery times and cost-effective last-mile delivery solutions.
- Target Industries: Focus on e-commerce retailers, healthcare providers, and food delivery services.

- Environmental Impact: Highlight the sustainability benefits of reducing carbon emissions from traditional delivery vehicles.

Requirements to Start:
- Drone Technology Expertise: Access to drone engineers and pilots skilled in autonomous flight and navigation.
- Regulatory Compliance: Obtain necessary permits and certifications from aviation authorities for drone operations.
- Safety Protocols: Implement safety measures to prevent accidents and ensure public acceptance of drone deliveries.

Challenges:
- Airspace Regulations: Adhering to airspace regulations and navigating restrictions in urban areas.
- Weather Conditions: Addressing challenges posed by adverse weather conditions on drone operations.
- Public Perception: Overcoming concerns about privacy and noise pollution associated with drone deliveries.

Scalability Opportunities:
- Expansion to New Markets: Scale drone delivery services to remote areas or regions with limited access to traditional logistics.
- Technology Integration: Integrate AI for route optimization and predictive maintenance of drone fleets.
- Partnerships: Collaborate with local businesses and government agencies to pilot drone delivery projects and gain regulatory support.

Roadmap:
1. Prototype Development: Build and test drone prototypes for payload capacity and operational efficiency.
2. Regulatory Approval: Obtain necessary permits and conduct trials to demonstrate safety and reliability.
3. Market Launch: Pilot drone delivery services in select markets and refine operations based on user feedback.
4. Scaling Operations: Expand drone fleet and operational capabilities to meet growing demand and expand service areas.

Further Resources:
- Drone Delivery: Regulatory Compliance and Best Practices
- Case Studies on Successful Drone Delivery Implementations

8. Biometric Security Solutions

Description: Develop biometric authentication and security solutions leveraging technologies such as fingerprint scanning, facial recognition, and voice authentication.

Marketing Insights and Opportunities:

- Security Enhancement: Biometrics offer enhanced security compared to traditional passwords and PINs.
- Industry Applications: Target sectors including banking, healthcare, and government for secure access control and identity verification.
- User Convenience: Highlight ease of use and quick authentication processes with biometric technologies.

Requirements to Start:
- Biometric Technology Expertise: Access to biometric engineers and cybersecurity experts skilled in developing secure authentication systems.
- Data Privacy: Implement encryption and secure storage protocols to protect biometric data from unauthorized access.
- Compliance: Ensure compliance with data protection regulations (e.g., GDPR, HIPAA) when handling biometric information.

Challenges:
- Accuracy and Reliability: Ensuring biometric systems accurately identify individuals under various conditions (e.g., lighting, facial expressions).
- Ethical Considerations: Addressing concerns related to privacy invasion and potential misuse of biometric data.
- Integration Complexity: Integrating biometric systems with existing IT infrastructure and legacy systems.

Scalability Opportunities:
- Multi-Factor Authentication: Expand biometric solutions to include multi-factor authentication for enhanced security layers.
- Global Adoption: Customize biometric solutions to comply with regional regulations and cultural preferences.
- Partnerships: Collaborate with technology providers and service integrators to deploy biometric solutions across different industries.

Roadmap:
1. Technology Assessment: Evaluate biometric technologies and select suitable modalities for different use cases.
2. Prototype Development: Build prototypes and conduct usability testing to validate accuracy and user acceptance.
3. Pilot Deployments: Partner with early adopters to pilot biometric solutions in real-world environments.
4. Market Expansion: Scale biometric offerings based on pilot results and market demand, focusing on scalability and reliability.

Further Resources:
- Biometric Security: Implementation Strategies and Case Studies
- Emerging Trends in Biometric Authentication

9. Digital Events Management Company

Description: Offer digital events management services, like a virtual space that can be custom decorated according to a real-life event, and attendees can see and manage their digital avatars while also digitally participating in activities like photoshoots, speeches, gatherings etc.

Marketing Insights and Opportunities:

- Growing demand for virtual events due to globalization, cost savings, and accessibility.

- Expansion into niche markets like corporate training, virtual trade shows, and online conferences.
  - Offering customizable digital avatars and immersive experiences to enhance participant engagement.

Requirements to Start:

- Reliable virtual event platform with features for avatar customization, real-time interactions, and secure data handling.

- High-speed internet and servers capable of handling multiple participants and virtual environments.
- Knowledge of virtual reality (VR), augmented reality (AR), and digital event management tools.
- Team with skills in 3D modeling, software development, and user experience (UX) design.
- Data protection measures compliant with international regulations.
  - Contracts and agreements for virtual event hosting, participant rights, and liabilities.

Challenges:

- Ensuring seamless user experience across different devices and internet speeds.

- Addressing glitches, latency issues, and server capacity during peak usage times.
- Educating potential clients about the benefits and capabilities of virtual events.
- Overcoming resistance to change and skepticism about virtual event effectiveness.
- Protecting participant data, preventing hacking, and ensuring virtual event integrity.
  - Compliance with data privacy laws and regulations.

Scalability Opportunities:

- Incorporating AI-driven analytics for personalized participant experiences.
- Enhancing VR/AR capabilities for more immersive and interactive virtual environments.
- Partnering with industries beyond corporate events (e.g., education, healthcare, entertainment).
- Offering hybrid event solutions that combine virtual and in-person experiences.
- Launching localized versions of the platform for international markets.
- Forming strategic alliances with global event organizers and technology firms.

Roadmap:

1. Define target audience segments and value propositions.
2. Develop MVP (Minimum Viable Product) of virtual event platform.
3. Build partnerships with technology providers and event organizers.
4. Conduct beta testing and gather user feedback.
5. Launch marketing campaigns to attract early adopters and build brand awareness.
6. Refine platform features based on user behavior and market response.
7. Scale infrastructure to support larger events and increased user traffic.

8. Expand service offerings (e.g., premium avatar features, virtual event consultancy).
9. Explore international markets and strategic partnerships for global expansion.

Further Resources:
- Online communities, forums, and webinars focusing on digital events, VR/AR, and event management.
- Courses on virtual event planning, VR/AR technologies, and digital marketing strategies.
- Webinars and workshops offered by tech firms, universities, and industry experts.
- Collaboration with VR/AR developers, digital agencies, and tech consultants specializing in virtual events.
- Outsourcing technical support, platform maintenance, and cybersecurity services.

10. Autonomous Vehicles for Last-Mile Delivery

Description: Develop autonomous vehicle solutions for last mile delivery of goods and packages, leveraging AI and robotics for efficient logistics operations.

Marketing Insights and Opportunities:
- Delivery Efficiency: Autonomous vehicles offer faster and more cost-effective last-mile delivery solutions compared to traditional methods.
- Urban Logistics: Address challenges in urban congestion and traffic management with autonomous delivery fleets.
- Sustainability: Promote eco-friendly delivery options by reducing carbon emissions from delivery vehicles.

Requirements to Start:
- Autonomous Vehicle Expertise: Access to robotics engineers and AI specialists skilled in autonomous navigation systems.
- Regulatory Compliance: Obtain permits and certifications for testing and deployment of autonomous vehicles in urban environments.
- Safety Standards: Implement safety protocols and collision avoidance systems to ensure pedestrian and road user safety.

Challenges:
- Technological Reliability: Ensuring reliability and performance of autonomous vehicle systems under varying weather and traffic conditions.
- Public Acceptance: Overcoming societal apprehensions and legal barriers related to autonomous vehicle adoption.
- Infrastructure Compatibility: Addressing infrastructure needs such as charging stations and vehicle maintenance hubs for autonomous fleets.

Scalability Opportunities:
- Global Deployment: Expand autonomous delivery services to metropolitan areas and international markets.
- Fleet Management: Develop AI-driven fleet management systems for optimizing delivery routes and vehicle utilization.
- Partnerships: Collaborate with e-commerce platforms, retailers, and logistics providers to integrate autonomous delivery solutions.

Roadmap:
1. Prototype Development: Build and test autonomous vehicle prototypes in controlled environments.
2. Pilot Programs: Conduct pilot programs in collaboration with local authorities and business partners to validate technology and gather feedback.
3. Regulatory Approval: Obtain regulatory approval for commercial deployment and scale operations based on pilot results.
4. Expansion Strategy: Expand autonomous delivery services strategically, focusing on scalability, safety, and operational efficiency.

Further Resources:
- Autonomous Vehicles: Challenges and Opportunities in Urban Logistics
- Case Studies on Autonomous Delivery Implementations

11. Cyber security Solutions for Small Businesses

Description: Provide comprehensive cyber security solutions tailored to the needs of small and medium-sized enterprises (SMEs) to protect against cyber threats and data breaches.

Marketing Insights and Opportunities:
- Security Demand: Increasing cyber security threats require SMEs to invest in robust protection measures.
- Compliance Requirements: Address regulatory compliance needs (e.g., GDPR, HIPAA) for data security and privacy.
- Cost-Effective Solutions: Offer affordable cyber security packages that fit within SME budgets without compromising protection.

Requirements to Start:
- Cyber security Expertise: Access to cyber security professionals skilled in threat detection, incident response, and network security.
- Security Tools: Invest in advanced cyber security software and hardware for threat prevention and detection.
- Customer Education: Provide training and awareness programs to educate SMEs on cybersecurity best practices and risks.

Challenges:
- Budget Constraints: SMEs may perceive cyber security investments as discretionary spending, impacting adoption rates.
- Resource Limitations: Overcoming resource constraints to implement and maintain effective cyber security measures.
- Cyber Insurance: Addressing complexities in cyber insurance coverage and risk mitigation strategies for SME clients.

Scalability Opportunities:
- Managed Security Services: Expand offerings to include managed security services (MSSP) for ongoing monitoring and threat management.

- Industry Specialization: Develop industry-specific cyber security solutions tailored to sectors such as healthcare, finance, and retail.
- Partnerships: Collaborate with IT service providers and industry associations to reach and support SME clients effectively.

Roadmap:
1. Assessment and Planning: Conduct cyber security assessments and develop customized security plans for SME clients.
2. Implementation: Deploy cyber security solutions and conduct staff training on security protocols and best practices.
3. Monitoring and Support: Provide 24/7 monitoring and incident response services to mitigate cyber threats proactively.
4. Compliance and Certification: Assist SME clients in achieving and maintaining industry certifications and regulatory compliance.

Further Resources:
- Cyber security for Small Businesses: Best Practices and Implementation Guides
- Case Studies on Effective Cyber security Measures for SMEs

12. Remote Healthcare Monitoring Solutions

Description: Develop remote healthcare monitoring solutions using IoT devices and telemedicine platforms to monitor patients' health remotely and provide timely medical intervention.

Marketing Insights and Opportunities:
- Healthcare Access: Improve access to healthcare services for patients in remote or underserved areas through remote monitoring.
- Chronic Disease Management: Support patients with chronic conditions by enabling continuous monitoring and early intervention.
- Aging Population: Address the growing demand for senior care solutions that allow aging adults to live independently while receiving medical oversight.

Requirements to Start:
- Healthcare Technology Expertise: Access to healthcare professionals and technology developers specializing in telemedicine and IoT.
- Device Integration: Develop IT devices and wearable capable of collecting and transmitting patient health data securely.
- Regulatory Compliance: Ensure compliance with healthcare regulations for patient data privacy and security.

Challenges:
- Data Interoperability: Integrating data from diverse IoT devices and health monitoring platforms into cohesive patient records.
- User Adoption: Educating patients and healthcare providers on the benefits and usage of remote monitoring technologies.
- Medical Liability: Addressing legal considerations and liability issues associated with remote healthcare monitoring and telemedicine.

Scalability Opportunities:
- Telehealth Expansion: Extend remote monitoring services to include virtual consultations and remote diagnostics.
- AI Integration: Incorporate AI algorithms for predictive analytics and personalized healthcare recommendations based on patient data.
- Partnerships: Collaborate with healthcare providers, insurers, and technology vendors to expand market reach and service offerings.

Roadmap:
1. Needs Assessment: Identify healthcare providers' and patients' needs for remote monitoring and telehealth services.
2. Technology Development: Design and prototype IoT devices and telemedicine platforms tailored to healthcare use cases.
3. Pilot Testing: Conduct trials with healthcare facilities and patient groups to validate technology and refine user interfaces.
4. Deployment and Support: Roll out remote monitoring solutions with ongoing technical support and training for healthcare professionals.

Further Resources:
- Remote Patient Monitoring: Implementation Strategies and Case Studies
- Telemedicine Trends and Innovations in Healthcare

Introduction to Retail and Ecommerce Businesses

Retail and ecommerce industries continue to evolve with technological advancements and changing consumer behaviors. From online marketplaces to niche subscription services, entrepreneurs have ample opportunities to innovate and cater to diverse customer demands. Successful ventures in this sector often blend creativity with customer-centric strategies, leveraging digital platforms to reach global audiences while offering personalized shopping experiences. Here are innovative business ideas poised to capitalize on emerging trends and consumer preferences:

13. Subscription Box Services

Description: Curate subscription boxes featuring niche products like beauty items, gourmet foods, or pet accessories, delivered monthly or quarterly to subscribers' doorsteps.

Marketing Insights and Opportunities:
- Subscription Economy: Capitalize on the growing trend of subscription-based services offering convenience and curated experiences.
- Targeted Marketing: Appeal to niche markets with specialized interests, such as vegan snacks, eco-friendly products, or luxury goods.
- Customer Loyalty: Build long-term relationships with subscribers through personalized offerings and exclusive discounts.

Requirements to Start:
- Product Sourcing: Establish partnerships with suppliers for unique and high-quality items suitable for subscription boxes.
- Logistics: Set up efficient shipping and fulfilment processes to ensure timely delivery and customer satisfaction.
- Marketing Strategy: Implement targeted digital marketing campaigns to attract and retain subscribers through social media and email marketing.

Challenges:
- Retention Rates: Maintain subscriber interest and reduce churn by consistently delivering value and novelty in each box.
- Inventory Management: Forecast demand accurately to manage inventory levels and prevent overstock or shortages.
- Competition: Stand out in a crowded market by offering distinctive themes, customization options, or sustainable packaging solutions.

Scalability Opportunities:
- Diversified Offerings: Expand subscription box themes to cater to different demographics and seasonal trends.
- Global Reach: Explore international shipping options to reach a broader audience and tap into global markets.

- Partnerships: Collaborate with influencers, brands, and subscription box aggregators to increase visibility and subscriber acquisition.

Roadmap:
1. Market Research: Identify target demographics and popular subscription box categories through consumer surveys and trend analysis.
2. Product Curation: Source and curate products that align with subscriber preferences and market trends.
3. Launch Strategy: Create compelling subscription plans, pricing models, and promotional offers to attract early adopters.
4. Feedback Loop: Gather feedback from subscribers to refine product offerings and improve customer satisfaction over time.

Further Resources:
- Subscription Box Business Models: Strategies for Success
- Case Studies on Successful Subscription Box Startups

14. Online Marketplace for Local Artisans

Description: Create an online platform where local artisans and craftsmen can showcase and sell handmade goods, fostering community support and artisanal craftsmanship.

Marketing Insights and Opportunities:
- Support Local: Tap into the growing consumer preference for ethically sourced and locally made products.
- Artisanal Storytelling: Highlight the stories and craftsmanship behind each product to resonate with conscious consumers.
- Community Engagement: Build a community-driven marketplace where customers can connect directly with artisans.

Requirements to Start:
- Artisan Network: Recruit and onboard local artisans skilled in various crafts such as pottery, jewellery making, or woodworking.
- E-commerce Platform: Develop a user-friendly website with robust features for product listings, transactions, and customer reviews.
- Brand Identity: Establish a brand that emphasises authenticity, quality, and the cultural significance of artisanal products.

Challenges:
- Marketplace Differentiation: Differentiate from mass-produced goods by focusing on unique, handmade items with artistic value.
- Logistics and Shipping: Coordinate logistics for product shipping and delivery, ensuring products reach customers safely and on time.
- Artisan Support: Provide resources and training to artisans on e-commerce best practices and product photography to enhance online visibility.

Scalability Opportunities:

- Expansion of Categories: Diversify product categories to include a wider range of artisanal goods and crafts.
- Regional Expansion: Partner with artisans from neighboring regions or countries to expand product diversity and geographic reach.
- Artisan Collaborations: Foster collaborations between artisans to create exclusive collections and limited-edition products for the marketplace.

Roadmap:
1. Artisan Outreach: Identify and onboard local artisans through craft fairs, community networks, and online outreach campaigns.
2. Platform Development: Build and customize the marketplace platform with intuitive navigation, secure payment systems, and mobile compatibility.
3. Marketing and Launch: Promote the marketplace through social media campaigns, local partnerships, and targeted advertising.
4. Community Building: Engage customers and artisans through storytelling, virtual events, and user-generated content to foster a supportive community.

Further Resources:
- Building a Successful Online Marketplace: Best Practices and Case Studies
- Supporting Local Artisans: Strategies for Sustainable Growth

15. Eco-Friendly Fashion Brand

Description: Launch a fashion brand committed to sustainability, offering eco-friendly clothing and accessories made from organic materials or recycled fabrics.

Marketing Insights and Opportunities:
- Ethical Fashion: Appeal to environmentally conscious consumers seeking sustainable alternatives to fast fashion.
- Transparency: Communicate the brand's commitment to ethical sourcing, fair trade practices, and eco-friendly production methods.
- Storytelling: Share the journey and impact of each product, from material sourcing to manufacturing, to resonate with mindful consumers.

Requirements to Start:
- Sustainable Supply Chain: Source organic fabrics, recycled materials, and eco-friendly dyes from certified suppliers and manufacturers.
- Brand Identity: Develop a brand identity that reflects sustainability values through product design, packaging, and marketing messages.
- Online Presence: Establish an e-commerce website with a focus on user experience, storytelling, and educational content on sustainable fashion.

Challenges:
- Cost of Sustainability: Manage higher production costs associated with eco-friendly materials and ethical labor practices.
- Consumer Education: Educate consumers about the environmental impact of fast fashion and the benefits of supporting sustainable brands.
- Competitive Market: Stand out in the competitive fashion industry by offering unique designs, quality craftsmanship, and transparent practices.

Scalability Opportunities:
- Capsule Collections: Launch seasonal collections and limited-edition pieces to generate excitement and attract fashion-forward consumers.
- International Expansion: Explore international markets and partnerships with retailers aligned with sustainability values.
- Collaborations: Partner with influencers, sustainability advocates, and fashion designers to expand brand reach and credibility.

Roadmap:
1. Market Research: Identify target demographics and consumer preferences for sustainable fashion through market analysis and trend research.
2. Product Development: Design and prototype eco-friendly clothing lines, ensuring quality, fit, and sustainability standards.
3. Brand Launch: Create a brand launch strategy with a focus on storytelling, social media campaigns, and influencer partnerships.
4. Customer Engagement: Build a loyal customer base through ongoing communication, feedback loops, and community-building initiatives centered around sustainability.

Further Resources:
- Sustainable Fashion: Trends and Strategies for Success
- Case Studies on Eco-Friendly Fashion Brands

These detailed descriptions provide comprehensive insights into each business idea under the "Retail and Ecommerce" sector, focusing on their potential, requirements, challenges, scalability opportunities, roadmap, and further resources. They aim to assist aspiring entrepreneurs in evaluating and implementing these innovative concepts effectively in the marketplace.

16. Personalized Gift Services

Description: Launch an online platform offering personalized gift options, including custom engraving, monogramming, and bespoke gift packages for various occasions.

Marketing Insights and Opportunities:
- Gift Personalization: Appeal to consumers seeking unique and meaningful gifts personalized with names, dates, or custom messages.
- Seasonal Demand: Capitalize on peak seasons such as holidays, birthdays, weddings, and corporate events for gift-giving.
- Corporate Gifting: Offer tailored solutions for businesses seeking personalized gifts for clients, employees, and partners.

Requirements to Start:
- Product Variety: Partner with suppliers and manufacturers capable of producing customizable items like jewelry, home decor, and apparel.
- E-commerce Platform: Develop a user-friendly website with intuitive design tools for customers to personalize and preview gifts.

- Marketing Strategy: Implement targeted marketing campaigns via social media, email newsletters, and influencer partnerships to reach gift-givers.

Challenges:
- Quality Control: Ensure high-quality craftsmanship and accurate customization to meet customer expectations.
- Order Fulfillment: Manage peak demand periods and ensure timely delivery of personalized gifts, especially during holidays.
- Customer Satisfaction: Address potential issues related to order customization, shipping delays, and product returns or exchanges.

Scalability Opportunities:
- Expansion of Product Lines: Introduce new customization options and gift categories to appeal to diverse customer preferences.
- Corporate Partnerships: Collaborate with event planners, corporations, and wedding planners to offer bulk orders and customized gifting solutions.
- International Shipping: Explore international markets and logistics solutions to expand the reach of personalized gift services globally.

Roadmap:
1. Market Research: Identify target demographics and consumer preferences for personalized gifts through surveys and competitor analysis.
2. Supplier Relationships: Establish partnerships with reliable suppliers and artisans capable of producing high-quality customized products.
3. Platform Development: Build and launch an intuitive e-commerce platform with robust customization features and secure payment gateways.
4. Customer Engagement: Implement personalized marketing strategies and customer support initiatives to build trust and loyalty among gift-givers.

Further Resources:
- Personalized Gift Market Trends and Case Studies
- Best Practices in Online Personalization and Customer Experience

17. Customized Meal Kit Delivery

Description: Offer personalized meal kit delivery services that cater to dietary preferences, allergies, and nutritional needs, providing convenient and healthy cooking solutions.

Marketing Insights and Opportunities:
- Convenience: Appeal to busy professionals and families seeking convenient meal preparation options without compromising on nutrition.
- Health and Wellness: Target health-conscious consumers with customizable meal plans focused on organic, gluten-free, or vegan diets.
- Subscription Model: Utilize subscription-based services to build recurring revenue and foster customer loyalty through regular meal deliveries.

Requirements to Start:

- Chef and Nutrition Expertise: Collaborate with chefs and nutritionists to develop balanced and diverse meal options tailored to customer preferences.
- Supply Chain Management: Source fresh ingredients from local farms and suppliers to ensure quality and sustainability.
- Packaging and Delivery: Invest in eco-friendly packaging solutions and reliable logistics partners for efficient meal kit delivery.

Challenges:
- Ingredient Availability: Manage seasonal fluctuations and ingredient sourcing challenges to maintain menu consistency.
- Customization Complexity: Develop a user-friendly platform for customers to customize meal preferences, portion sizes, and delivery schedules.
- Competitive Pricing: Balance meal kit costs with customer expectations for value, quality, and convenience.

Scalability Opportunities:
- Menu Expansion: Introduce new recipes and dietary options based on customer feedback and culinary trends.
- Regional Expansion: Expand delivery services to new cities and regions to reach a broader customer base.
- Partnerships: Collaborate with fitness centers, nutritionists, and corporate wellness programs to promote healthy eating habits and personalized meal plans.

Roadmap:
1. Menu Development: Create a diverse menu of customizable meal options, considering dietary preferences and nutritional guidelines.
2. Platform Development: Build an intuitive online platform or mobile app for customers to select meals, customize orders, and manage subscriptions.
3. Operations Setup: Establish kitchen facilities, food preparation processes, and packaging standards compliant with health and safety regulations.
4. Marketing and Launch: Launch targeted marketing campaigns, including social media promotions, influencer partnerships, and sampling programs to attract early adopters.

Further Resources:
- Meal Kit Delivery Market Trends and Consumer Preferences
- Case Studies on Successful Meal Kit Startups

18. Vintage and Retro Clothing Store

Description: Launch an online store specializing in curated collections of vintage and retro fashion, offering timeless apparel, accessories, and footwear.

Marketing Insights and Opportunities:
- Nostalgia Appeal: Attract fashion enthusiasts and collectors drawn to iconic styles from past decades, such as 1960s mod fashion or 1980s street wear.
- Sustainability Focus: Promote eco-conscious shopping habits by offering pre-loved clothing and reducing fashion industry waste.

- Fashion Events: Participate in virtual and physical vintage fashion markets, pop-up shops, and themed events to showcase curated collections.

Requirements to Start:
- Vintage Sourcing: Establish partnerships with suppliers, thrift stores, and collectors to source high-quality vintage clothing and accessories.
- Online Storefront: Develop a visually appealing e-commerce website with intuitive navigation, detailed product descriptions, and secure checkout options.
- Brand Curation: Curate collections that reflect distinct eras, styles, and fashion trends while ensuring authenticity and quality.

Challenges:
- Inventory Management: Manage inventory turnover and ensure a steady supply of unique vintage pieces to meet customer demand.
- Customer Fit: Address sizing inconsistencies and provide detailed measurements and fit guides for vintage apparel.
- Competition: Differentiate from mass-market retailers and other vintage sellers by offering rare finds, impeccable curation, and excellent customer service.

Scalability Opportunities:
- Online Community Building: Engage with vintage fashion enthusiasts through social media, blog content and online forums.
- Global Reach: Expand market reach through international shipping and digital marketing strategies targeting global vintage fashion enthusiasts.
- Collaborations: Partner with fashion influencers, stylists, and media outlets to increase brand visibility and attract new customers.

Roadmap:
1. Market Research: Identify target demographics and consumer preferences for vintage fashion through trend analysis and customer surveys.
2. Supplier Relationships: Build relationships with reliable vintage suppliers and collectors to access unique and high-demand inventory.
3. Website Development: Design and launch an e-commerce platform optimized for vintage shopping experiences, including mobile compatibility and secure transactions.
4. Marketing Strategy: Implement targeted marketing campaigns, including SEO, social media advertising, and email newsletters to attract vintage fashion enthusiasts and collectors.

Further Resources:
- Vintage Fashion Market Trends and Consumer Insights
- Strategies for Launching and Growing an Online Vintage Store

These detailed descriptions provide comprehensive insights into each business idea under the "Retail and Ecommerce" sector, focusing on their potential, requirements, challenges, scalability opportunities, roadmap, and further resources. They aim to assist aspiring entrepreneurs in evaluating and implementing these innovative concepts effectively in the marketplace.

20. Organic and Natural Beauty Products E-commerce Platform

Description: Launch an e-commerce platform offering a wide range of organic and natural beauty products, including skincare, hair care, and cosmetics, promoting health-conscious beauty solutions.

Marketing Insights and Opportunities:
- Health and Wellness Trends: Cater to consumers seeking clean beauty alternatives free from harmful chemicals and artificial ingredients.
- Educational Content: Provide product transparency and educate consumers about the benefits of organic ingredients and sustainable packaging.
- Personalization: Offer personalized skincare routines and beauty regimens based on individual skin types and concerns.

Requirements to Start:
- Product Sourcing: Partner with certified organic suppliers and eco-friendly brands committed to sustainable practices and cruelty-free production.
- E-commerce Infrastructure: Develop a secure and user-friendly online store with intuitive navigation, detailed product descriptions, and customer reviews.
- Brand Curation: Curate a selection of premium organic brands and products that align with your platform's values of health, sustainability, and effectiveness.

Challenges:
- Regulatory Compliance: Navigate regulations governing organic certification, product labeling, and international shipping restrictions.
- Market Differentiation: Stand out in a competitive beauty industry by emphasizing unique selling points such as ingredient quality, product efficacy, and ethical sourcing.
- Customer Trust: Build trust and credibility through transparent communication, customer reviews, and endorsements from beauty influencers and dermatologists.

Scalability Opportunities:
- Product Expansion: Expand product offerings to include new categories such as organic perfumes, bath products, and men's grooming essentials.
- Global Reach: Implement international shipping and localization strategies to reach beauty enthusiasts worldwide.
- Subscription Services: Introduce beauty subscription boxes or recurring delivery options for replenishable products and seasonal beauty routines.

Roadmap:
1. Market Analysis: Conduct market research to identify consumer preferences, competitive landscape, and emerging trends in organic beauty.
2. Supplier Partnerships: Establish relationships with reputable suppliers and negotiate agreements for product exclusivity and bulk purchasing.
3. Website Development: Design and launch an e-commerce platform optimized for mobile devices with secure payment gateways and customer support features.
4. Marketing Campaigns: Launch targeted digital marketing campaigns, influencer collaborations, and social media promotions to attract health-conscious consumers.

Further Resources:
- Organic Beauty Industry Trends and Consumer Insights
- Best Practices for Launching an E-commerce Beauty Platform

21. Specialty Tea and Coffee Subscription Service

Description: Create a subscription service offering curated selections of specialty teas and coffees sourced from around the world, delivering unique flavors and brewing experiences to subscribers.

Marketing Insights and Opportunities:
- Gourmet Experience: Appeal to tea and coffee enthusiasts seeking exotic blends, single-origin varieties, and artisanal roasts.
- Gift Market: Target gift-giving occasions with subscription options suitable for birthdays, holidays, and corporate gifting.
- Educational Content: Provide brewing tips, flavor profiles, and origin stories to enhance subscriber appreciation and engagement.

Requirements to Start:
- Supplier Relationships: Establish partnerships with tea estates, coffee roasters, and importers to access premium and exclusive varieties.
- Subscription Platform: Develop a subscription management system for customizable plans, recurring billing, and flexible delivery schedules.
- Packaging and Presentation: Design eco-friendly packaging that preserves freshness and enhances the aesthetic appeal of specialty teas and coffees.

Challenges:
- Supply Chain Management: Ensure consistent supply and quality control of seasonal tea and coffee batches from international suppliers.
- Customer Acquisition: Educate consumers about the value of specialty teas and coffees through tasting events, sample packs, and online promotions.
- Subscription Retention: Maintain subscriber interest and reduce churn by offering personalized recommendations, limited editions, and subscriber perks.

Scalability Opportunities:
- Product Diversification: Expand product offerings to include accessories such as brewing equipment, mugs, and gift sets tailored to tea and coffee lovers.
- Corporate Partnerships: Collaborate with cafes, restaurants, and hospitality businesses for wholesale and corporate subscription programs.
- Market Expansion: Enter new markets through partnerships with international distributors and online marketplaces specializing in gourmet food and beverages.

Roadmap:
1. Product Selection: Curate initial tea and coffee selections based on market research, consumer feedback, and supplier capabilities.
2. Subscription Model: Develop subscription tiers with customizable options for tea types, coffee roasts, and frequency of deliveries.
3. Website Launch: Design and launch an e-commerce website with a focus on user experience, subscription management, and educational content.

4. Marketing Strategy: Implement targeted marketing campaigns, SEO optimization, and social media engagement to attract early adopters and build brand awareness.

Further Resources:
- Specialty Tea and Coffee Market Trends and Insights
- Strategies for Building a Successful Subscription Service

22. Customized Furniture Design and Sales Platform

Description: Establish an online platform offering customized furniture design services, allowing customers to personalize furniture pieces based on style, dimensions, and materials.

Marketing Insights and Opportunities:
- Personalization Trend: Appeal to homeowners and interior designers seeking bespoke furniture solutions tailored to specific aesthetic preferences and space requirements.
- Home Improvement Market: Target consumers investing in home renovations, redecorations, and personalized living spaces.
- Collaborative Design: Engage customers in the design process, offering customization options such as upholstery fabrics, wood finishes, and ergonomic features.

Requirements to Start:
- Design Expertise: Employ skilled furniture designers and craftsmen capable of translating customer visions into functional and stylish furniture pieces.
- Supply Chain Management: Partner with manufacturers and suppliers to source high-quality materials and ensure craftsmanship standards meet customer expectations.
- Online Platform: Develop a user-friendly website with 3D modeling tools, virtual room planners, and secure payment gateways for seamless customer interactions.

Challenges:
- Production Logistics: Manage production timelines, shipping logistics, and quality assurance for custom furniture orders.
- Customer Expectations: Balance design flexibility with production constraints to deliver customized furniture that meets quality standards and customer timelines.
- Competitive Pricing: Price customization options competitively while maintaining profitability and perceived value in the custom furniture market.

Scalability Opportunities:
- Product Expansion: Introduce new furniture categories, styles, and design collections based on market trends and customer feedback.
- B2B Partnerships: Collaborate with interior designers, real estate developers, and hospitality businesses for bulk orders and custom project installations.
- Digital Innovation: Invest in augmented reality (AR) technology for virtual furniture placement and visualization tools to enhance the online shopping experience.

Roadmap:

1. Market Research: Identify target demographics, consumer preferences, and competitive landscape in the custom furniture market.
2. Design Consultation: Offer personalized design consultations and mock-ups to prospective customers to showcase customization capabilities.
3. Website Development: Build and launch an e-commerce platform with comprehensive product galleries, customization options, and customer support features.
4. Marketing and Outreach: Implement targeted marketing strategies, including digital advertising, content marketing, and partnerships with home decor influencers and industry publications.

Further Resources:
- Custom Furniture Design Trends and Customer Insights
- Best Practices for Launching an E-commerce Furniture Platform

Introduction to Services and Consulting Businesses

Services and consulting businesses play a crucial role in supporting industries and individuals with specialized expertise, operational efficiencies, and tailored solutions. From virtual assistance to sustainable event planning, these ventures offer personalized services that optimize productivity, enhance organizational effectiveness, and promote sustainable practices. Successful enterprises in this sector leverage innovation, client-centric strategies, and industry insights to deliver measurable results and build long-term partnerships.

23. Virtual Personal Assistant Services

Description: Provide virtual personal assistant services to individuals, entrepreneurs, and businesses, offering administrative support, scheduling assistance, and task management remotely.

Marketing Insights and Opportunities:
- Remote Work Trends: Capitalize on the rise of remote work and freelance economy by offering flexible and scalable virtual assistant solutions.
- Specialized Services: Differentiate by offering niche services such as social media management, travel coordination, and inbox management tailored to client needs.
- Time Management: Position services as time-saving solutions for busy professionals and executives seeking to delegate non-core tasks effectively.

Requirements to Start:
- Skill Set: Recruit virtual assistants proficient in administrative tasks, communication skills, and digital tools such as project management software and calendar apps.
- Technology Infrastructure: Implement secure communication channels, cloud-based storage solutions, and virtual collaboration platforms for seamless service delivery.
- Client Onboarding: Develop streamlined processes for client intake, needs assessment, and service customization to meet diverse client requirements.

Challenges:
- Client Trust: Build credibility and trust through transparent communication, confidentiality agreements, and timely task completion.
- Workflow Management: Establish efficient workflows and task prioritization methods to manage multiple client projects and deadlines effectively.
- Service Differentiation: Showcase expertise in specialized services and industry-specific knowledge to attract clients seeking tailored virtual assistant solutions.

Scalability Opportunities:
- Service Expansion: Diversify service offerings to include specialized virtual assistant packages for industries such as healthcare, legal, and creative sectors.

- Global Reach: Leverage remote service capabilities to expand clientele beyond local markets through digital marketing, referrals, and strategic partnerships.
- Automation Integration: Incorporate AI-driven tools and automation solutions to enhance service efficiency, task delegation, and client satisfaction.

Roadmap:
1. Market Research: Identify target markets, client demographics, and industry trends to tailor virtual assistant services and pricing models.
2. Talent Acquisition: Recruit and train virtual assistants with skills aligned with client needs, emphasizing reliability, professionalism, and adaptability.
3. Technology Implementation: Invest in secure IT infrastructure, software licenses, and virtual communication tools to support remote service delivery.
4. Marketing Strategy: Launch targeted marketing campaigns, social media outreach, and networking events to attract clients and establish industry partnerships.

Further Resources:
- Virtual Assistant Industry Trends and Best Practices
- Case Studies on Successful Virtual Assistant Businesses

24. Business Efficiency Consulting

Description: Offer business efficiency consulting services to help organizations streamline operations, optimize processes, and improve productivity and profitability.

Marketing Insights and Opportunities:
- Operational Excellence: Position services as solutions for cost reduction, resource optimization, and performance improvement across industries.
- Industry Expertise: Demonstrate specialized knowledge in areas such as supply chain management, IT systems integration, and workflow automation.
- Return on Investment: Highlight measurable outcomes and ROI metrics achieved through consulting interventions and process enhancements.

Requirements to Start:
- Consulting Expertise: Build a team of consultants with experience in process analysis, change management, and business strategy development.
- Client Engagement: Develop consulting frameworks, methodologies, and assessment tools tailored to client needs and industry benchmarks.
- Data Analytics: Utilize data-driven insights and performance metrics to identify inefficiencies, prioritize improvement opportunities, and track project outcomes.

Challenges:
- Client Resistance: Overcome organizational inertia and resistance to change by demonstrating the value proposition of efficiency consulting through case studies and testimonials.
- Competitive Landscape: Differentiate from competitors by offering customized solutions, industry specialization, and proven track record of successful client engagements.
- Project Scope Management: Define clear project scopes, deliverables, and timelines to manage client expectations and ensure project profitability.

Scalability Opportunities:
- Industry Verticals: Expand service offerings to target specific industries such as healthcare, manufacturing, and financial services with tailored consulting solutions.
- Global Expansion: Enter new markets through strategic partnerships, international certifications, and digital marketing campaigns targeting multinational corporations.
- Technology Integration: Leverage emerging technologies such as AI, IoT, and predictive analytics to enhance consulting services and deliver actionable insights to clients.

Roadmap:
1. Market Analysis: Conduct industry research, competitor analysis, and client interviews to identify pain points, market gaps, and consulting opportunities.
2. Consulting Framework: Develop proprietary methodologies, toolkits, and best practices for assessing organizational efficiency and recommending improvement strategies.
3. Client Acquisition: Build a strong client portfolio through networking, referrals, thought leadership content, and participation in industry conferences and seminars.
4. Performance Measurement: Implement performance metrics, KPI dashboards, and client feedback mechanisms to measure consulting impact and drive continuous improvement.

Further Resources:
- Business Efficiency Consulting Strategies and Case Studies
- Tools and Techniques for Operational Excellence

25. Sustainable Event Planning

Description: Provide event planning and management services with a focus on sustainability, offering eco-friendly venues, green catering options, and carbon-neutral event solutions.

Marketing Insights and Opportunities:
- Environmental Consciousness: Appeal to corporate clients, nonprofits, and individuals seeking sustainable event alternatives aligned with CSR goals and eco-friendly values.
- Green Certifications: Obtain certifications and partnerships with sustainable vendors, venues, and suppliers to enhance credibility and attract environmentally conscious clients.
- Community Engagement: Collaborate with local communities, environmental organizations, and eco-friendly brands to promote sustainable event practices and initiatives.

Requirements to Start:
- Vendor Partnerships: Establish relationships with sustainable vendors, caterers, florists, and venues committed to eco-friendly practices and carbon footprint reduction.
- Event Planning Expertise: Build a team of event planners skilled in sustainable event design, logistics management, and environmental impact assessment.

- Regulatory Compliance: Navigate local regulations, permits, and sustainability standards governing event planning and waste management practices.

Challenges:
- Cost Management: Manage additional costs associated with sustainable event components such as organic catering, eco-friendly decor, and waste diversion services.
- Client Education: Educate clients on the benefits of sustainable event practices, ROI of eco-friendly investments, and long-term environmental impact reduction.
- Logistical Coordination: Coordinate logistics for sustainable transportation, energy-efficient lighting, and waste reduction strategies to minimize event carbon footprint.

Scalability Opportunities:
- Event Portfolio Diversification: Expand service offerings to include virtual events, hybrid conferences, and sustainable team-building activities tailored to diverse client needs.
- Destination Events: Offer destination event planning services with an emphasis on sustainable travel, local community engagement, and cultural preservation.
- Corporate Partnerships: Form alliances with corporate sponsors, green initiatives, and sustainability-focused organizations to promote sustainable event planning services globally.

Roadmap:
1. Market Research: Identify target markets, client preferences, and industry trends in sustainable event planning through surveys, market analysis, and competitor benchmarking.
2. Supplier Network: Build a network of sustainable vendors, venues, and partners aligned with eco-friendly practices and event sustainability certifications.
3. Event Design: Develop sustainable event design concepts, green catering menus, and carbon offsetting strategies tailored to client event themes and objectives.
4. Marketing Strategy: Launch targeted marketing campaigns, digital outreach, and thought leadership content to position as a leader in sustainable event planning and attract environmentally conscious clients.

Further Resources:
- Sustainable Event Planning Best Practices and Case Studies
- Tools and Technologies for Green Event Management

26. Freelance Writing and Editing Services

Description: Offer freelance writing and editing services to businesses, authors, and content creators, providing high-quality content creation, editing, and proofreading solutions.

Marketing Insights and Opportunities:
- Content Demand: Address the growing demand for engaging and SEO-optimized content across digital platforms, blogs, and social media channels.
- Niche Expertise: Specialize in industry-specific content such as technical writing, copywriting, ghostwriting, and editorial services tailored to client requirements.

- Content Marketing: Position services as integral to client branding, thought leadership, and customer engagement strategies through compelling storytelling and persuasive communication.

Requirements to Start:
- Writing Portfolio: Showcase a diverse portfolio of writing samples, case studies, and client testimonials demonstrating proficiency in different content types and industries.
- Digital Presence: Establish an online presence through a professional website, blog, and social media profiles to attract clients and showcase expertise.
- Collaboration Tools: Utilize project management software, cloud-based platforms, and communication tools for seamless client collaboration and workflow management.

Challenges:
- Client Acquisition: Build a robust client base through networking, referrals, content marketing, and participation in industry forums and freelance marketplaces.
- Content Quality: Maintain high standards of writing, editing, and proofreading to meet client expectations for accuracy, clarity, and adherence to brand voice.
- Time Management: Balance multiple projects, deadlines, and client revisions while maintaining quality and timely delivery of content services.

Scalability Opportunities:
- Service Expansion: Diversify service offerings to include content strategy consulting, SEO optimization, and localization services for global audiences.
- Industry Partnerships: Collaborate with marketing agencies, web developers, and digital publishers to offer integrated content solutions and expand market reach.
- Training and Development: Hire additional writers, editors, and content specialists to scale operations and meet growing client demand for content creation and management.

Roadmap:
1. Market Analysis: Identify target markets, content preferences, and industry trends through competitor analysis, client surveys, and keyword research.
2. Service Packages: Develop customizable service packages, pricing models, and subscription plans aligned with client budgets and content marketing goals.
3. Client Relationships: Cultivate long-term relationships with clients through personalized communication, proactive project management, and ongoing content strategy support.
4. Marketing Strategy: Implement targeted marketing campaigns, SEO optimization, and thought leadership content to attract clients, demonstrate expertise, and build industry credibility.

Further Resources:
- Freelance Writing and Editing Best Practices
- Tools and Technologies for Content Creation and Management

27. Career Coaching and Resume Writing

Description: Provide career coaching and resume writing services to professionals and job seekers, offering personalized career development guidance, interview preparation, and resume optimization.

Marketing Insights and Opportunities:
- Job Market Trends: Address career transitions, job search challenges, and skill development needs in competitive job markets through tailored coaching and resume writing services.
- Professional Branding: Position services as essential for personal branding, career advancement, and job application success through impactful resumes, LinkedIn profiles, and interview coaching.
- Industry Expertise: Specialize in specific industries, career levels, and job roles to cater to diverse client needs and employment opportunities.

Requirements to Start:
- Coaching Certification: Obtain coaching certifications, credentials, or relevant training in career development, counseling, or human resources management.
- Resume Portfolio: Showcase a portfolio of successful resume examples, client testimonials, and career coaching case studies demonstrating proven results and client satisfaction.
- Client Assessment Tools: Implement career assessment tools, personality tests, and skills inventories to evaluate client strengths, career goals, and professional aspirations.

Challenges:
- Client Trust and Confidentiality: Build trust and maintain confidentiality while discussing sensitive career information, job search strategies, and personal branding efforts.
- Competitive Differentiation: Differentiate services through personalized coaching methodologies, industry insights, and client-centric approach to career development.
- Client Success Metrics: Measure client outcomes, job placement rates, and career advancement milestones to showcase service effectiveness and ROI for career coaching and resume writing services.

Scalability Opportunities:
- Service Expansion: Expand service offerings to include executive coaching, leadership development, and specialized career workshops for niche industries and professional certifications.
- Corporate Partnerships: Collaborate with corporations, educational institutions, and professional associations to offer career transition services, outplacement support, and employee career development programs.
- Digital Learning: Develop online courses, webinars, and career resources to reach global audiences and provide ongoing career guidance and professional development opportunities.

Roadmap:
1. Market Research: Identify target demographics, career challenges, and industry trends through client surveys, career fairs, and industry networking events.

2. Service Packages: Develop customizable coaching programs, resume writing packages, and interview preparation workshops tailored to client career goals and job search objectives.
3. Client Engagement: Build rapport and trust through initial consultations, goal-setting sessions, and progress reviews to tailor coaching strategies and resume writing services to individual client needs.
4. Marketing Strategy: Implement targeted marketing campaigns, SEO optimization, and content marketing initiatives to attract clients, enhance online visibility, and establish thought leadership in career coaching and resume writing.

Further Resources:
- Career Coaching Best Practices and Success Stories
- Tools and Techniques for Resume Writing and Personal Branding

28. Digital Marketing Agency

Description: Establish a digital marketing agency offering comprehensive services including SEO, PPC advertising, social media marketing, content creation, and website development.

Marketing Insights and Opportunities:
- Digital Transformation: Assist businesses in transitioning to digital platforms, enhancing online visibility, and driving customer acquisition through targeted digital marketing strategies.
- Data-Driven Marketing: Utilize analytics tools, customer insights, and performance metrics to optimize campaign effectiveness, ROI, and conversion rates for clients.
- Industry Specialization: Focus on niche industries, local markets, and emerging trends to deliver customized digital marketing solutions and competitive advantage.

Requirements to Start:
- Digital Expertise: Build a team of digital marketers, SEO specialists, content creators, and web developers proficient in digital marketing tools, platforms, and best practices.
- Technology Infrastructure: Invest in marketing automation software, CRM systems, and analytics tools to streamline campaign management, client reporting, and performance tracking.
- Client Acquisition Strategy: Develop a scalable sales pipeline, lead generation tactics, and client referral programs to attract businesses seeking digital marketing expertise.

Challenges:
- Market Competition: Navigate competitive landscape, industry consolidation, and evolving digital marketing trends to differentiate agency services and maintain client satisfaction.
- Client Retention: Demonstrate ROI, campaign success, and continuous improvement through data-driven insights, performance benchmarks, and client reporting transparency.

- Talent Acquisition and Training: Recruit and retain digital marketing talent with expertise in SEO, PPC advertising, social media management, and content marketing to support client campaigns and agency growth.

Scalability Opportunities:
- Service Expansion: Expand service offerings to include emerging technologies such as AI-driven marketing solutions, video marketing, and influencer partnerships to meet client demands and industry trends.
- Global Reach: Leverage digital platforms, international partnerships, and localization strategies to serve global clients and expand agency presence in new markets.
- Client Success Stories: Showcase client case studies, testimonials, and industry awards to build agency credibility, attract new clients, and retain existing client relationships.

Roadmap:
1. Market Analysis: Conduct market research, competitor analysis, and client surveys to identify industry trends, client pain points, and digital marketing opportunities.
2. Service Portfolio: Develop comprehensive service packages, pricing models, and customizable solutions aligned with client budgets, business goals, and digital marketing objectives.
3. Client On boarding: Implement streamlined on boarding processes, discovery workshops, and digital audits to assess client needs, establish KPIs, and develop tailored marketing strategies.
4. Marketing Strategy: Launch targeted digital marketing campaigns, thought leadership content, and industry partnerships to build agency brand awareness, attract qualified leads, and drive client acquisition.

Further Resources:
- Digital Marketing Trends and Innovations
- Tools and Technologies for Digital Agency Success

These detailed descriptions provide comprehensive insights into each business idea under the "Services and Consulting" sector, focusing on their potential, requirements, challenges, scalability opportunities, roadmap, and further resources. They aim to assist aspiring entrepreneurs in evaluating and implementing these innovative concepts effectively in the marketplace.

29. Social Media Management Consulting

Description: Offer social media management consulting services to businesses, helping them enhance their online presence, engage with their target audience, and drive brand awareness through strategic social media strategies.

Marketing Insights and Opportunities:
- Digital Engagement: Address the growing need for businesses to establish and maintain a strong social media presence, leveraging platforms like Facebook, Instagram, LinkedIn, and Twitter.

- Content Strategy: Develop customized content calendars, campaign ideas, and influencer collaborations to optimize engagement and reach target demographics effectively.
- Analytics and ROI: Utilize social media analytics tools to track performance metrics, measure ROI, and optimize campaigns based on data-driven insights.

Requirements to Start:
- Social Media Expertise: Build a team of social media managers, content creators, and analysts with proficiency in platform algorithms, content trends, and audience behavior.
- Client Assessment: Conduct social media audits, competitor analysis, and client consultations to understand business goals, brand voice, and target audience demographics.
- Technology Integration: Implement social media management tools, scheduling platforms, and analytics dashboards to streamline campaign execution, monitoring, and reporting.

Challenges:
- Platform Algorithm Changes: Stay updated with social media algorithm updates, policy changes, and best practices to maintain campaign effectiveness and audience engagement.
- Content Personalization: Create tailored content strategies, ad campaigns, and community management tactics to resonate with diverse audience segments and maximize organic reach.
- Client Education: Educate clients on social media ROI, performance metrics, and strategic growth opportunities to foster long-term partnerships and client satisfaction.

Scalability Opportunities:
- Service Expansion: Offer additional services such as paid advertising management, influencer marketing, and crisis management to meet evolving client needs and industry trends.
- Industry Specialization: Focus on niche markets, industries, or geographic regions to develop specialized social media strategies that align with client objectives and market dynamics.
- Automation and AI: Incorporate AI-driven tools, chat bots, and predictive analytics to enhance social media campaign automation, customer engagement, and conversion rate optimization.

Roadmap:
1. Market Analysis: Identify target industries, client personas, and competitive landscape through market research, industry reports, and social media trend analysis.
2. Service Offerings: Develop customized service packages, pricing models, and service level agreements (SLAs) tailored to client budgets, campaign objectives, and KPIs.
3. Client Acquisition: Implement lead generation strategies, networking events, and referral programs to attract businesses seeking social media management consulting services.
4. Continuous Improvement: Monitor campaign performance, conduct A/B testing, and adapt strategies based on real-time data insights to optimize social media ROI and client satisfaction.

Further Resources:
- Social Media Marketing Trends and Best Practices
- Tools and Technologies for Social Media Management

30. Human Resources Outsourcing Services

Description: Provide human resources outsourcing services to businesses, offering HR administration, payroll processing, talent acquisition, employee relations, and compliance management solutions.

Marketing Insights and Opportunities:
- Operational Efficiency: Help businesses streamline HR functions, reduce administrative burdens, and focus on core business activities through outsourced HR services.
- Compliance Expertise: Ensure regulatory compliance, labor law adherence, and HR best practices to mitigate legal risks and maintain employee relations standards.
- Scalable Solutions: Offer scalable HR solutions tailored to small, medium, and large enterprises, adapting service levels and support based on organizational growth and workforce dynamics.

Requirements to Start:
- HR Expertise: Build a team of HR professionals, certified HR specialists, and payroll administrators with expertise in labor regulations, employment law, and HRIS systems.
- Service Infrastructure: Invest in HR software, cloud-based platforms, and secure data management systems to ensure confidentiality, data security, and compliance with client HR policies.
- Client Engagement: Conduct HR assessments, workforce audits, and organizational needs analyses to customize HR outsourcing solutions aligned with client objectives and business goals.

Challenges:
- Client Confidentiality: Maintain confidentiality, data privacy, and ethical standards while handling sensitive HR information, payroll records, and employee documentation.
- Service Quality Assurance: Establish service level agreements (SLAs), performance metrics, and client feedback mechanisms to measure service delivery, client satisfaction, and continuous improvement.
- Competitive Differentiation: Differentiate through industry specialization, customized HR solutions, and proactive HR advisory services that address specific client pain points and workforce challenges.

Scalability Opportunities:
- Service Expansion: Expand service offerings to include HR consulting, leadership development, training programs, and organizational development initiatives to support client growth and talent management strategies.

- Geographic Expansion: Enter new markets, industries, or geographic regions through strategic partnerships, acquisitions, and local market expertise to broaden client reach and service capabilities.
- Technology Integration: Leverage AI-driven HR analytics, predictive modeling, and workforce planning tools to optimize HR outsourcing services, talent acquisition strategies, and employee engagement initiatives.

Roadmap:
1. Market Research: Identify target industries, client demographics, and HR outsourcing trends through industry reports, client surveys, and competitor analysis.
2. Service Portfolio: Develop comprehensive HR service packages, pricing models, and service bundling options tailored to client needs, industry benchmarks, and regulatory requirements.
3. Client Acquisition: Implement lead generation strategies, client referrals, and industry networking events to attract businesses seeking HR outsourcing solutions and HR advisory services.
4. Service Excellence: Establish quality assurance processes, client satisfaction surveys, and continuous improvement initiatives to enhance service delivery, client retention, and competitive advantage.

Further Resources:
- HR Outsourcing Best Practices and Case Studies
- Tools and Technologies for HR Management and Compliance

31. Market Research and Analysis Firm

Description: Establish a market research and analysis firm offering customized research solutions, competitive intelligence, consumer insights, and industry trend analysis to businesses.

Marketing Insights and Opportunities:
- Data-Driven Decision Making: Assist businesses in making informed decisions, market entry strategies, and product development initiatives based on market research findings and competitive analysis.
- Industry Expertise: Develop specialized research capabilities in sectors such as healthcare, technology, consumer goods, and financial services to deliver actionable insights and strategic recommendations.
- Thought Leadership: Position as industry thought leaders through white papers, industry reports, and conference presentations that showcase expertise in market research methodologies and data analysis techniques.

Requirements to Start:
- Research Expertise: Build a team of market researchers, data analysts, statisticians, and industry specialists with experience in qualitative and quantitative research methodologies.
- Research Tools: Invest in research tools, survey platforms, data visualization software, and statistical analysis programs to collect, analyze, and interpret market data effectively.

- Client Collaboration: Collaborate closely with clients to define research objectives, methodology frameworks, and deliverables that address specific business challenges and strategic goals.

Challenges:
- Data Accuracy and Reliability: Ensure data integrity, sample representativeness, and research methodology transparency to maintain credibility and deliver accurate market insights to clients.
- Competitive Intelligence: Navigate competitive landscape, industry dynamics, and emerging trends to provide clients with actionable competitive intelligence and market positioning strategies.
- Client Engagement: Foster collaborative partnerships, client trust, and long-term relationships through personalized service delivery, strategic advisory, and continuous research support.

Scalability Opportunities:
- Service Expansion: Expand research offerings to include custom research reports, industry benchmarking studies, market segmentation analysis, and predictive analytics solutions tailored to client needs.
- Global Reach: Develop international research capabilities, regional expertise, and multi-country studies to support global expansion strategies and client operations in diverse markets.
- Digital Transformation: Leverage AI-driven analytics, machine learning algorithms, and big data solutions to enhance research capabilities, data processing efficiency, and predictive modeling accuracy.

Roadmap:
1. Market Analysis: Conduct industry analysis, client needs assessments, and competitive benchmarking to identify market research opportunities, client pain points, and industry gaps.
2. Research Methodologies: Develop proprietary research methodologies, survey frameworks, and data collection techniques aligned with client objectives, industry standards, and best practices.
3. Client Acquisition: Implement targeted marketing campaigns, thought leadership content, and industry networking initiatives to attract clients, showcase research capabilities, and establish credibility in the market.
4. Research Excellence: Monitor research trends, quality assurance metrics, and client feedback to continuously improve research methodologies, deliverables, and client satisfaction.

Further Resources:
- Market Research Best Practices and Innovations
- Tools and Technologies for Data Analysis and Market Insights

These detailed descriptions provide comprehensive insights into each business idea under the "Services and consulting" sector, focusing on their potential, requirements, challenges, scalability opportunities, roadmap, and further resources. They aim to assist aspiring entrepreneurs in evaluating and implementing these innovative concepts effectively in the marketplace.

32. Legal Consulting for Startups and Small Businesses

Description: Provide legal consulting services tailored to startups and small businesses, offering legal advice, contract drafting, compliance assistance, intellectual property protection, and business formation guidance.

Marketing Insights and Opportunities:
- Startup Ecosystem: Address legal challenges and regulatory compliance issues specific to startups, entrepreneurs, and small business owners navigating initial growth stages.
- Industry Expertise: Specialize in industries such as technology, healthcare, e-commerce, and fintech to offer customized legal solutions aligned with client business models and operational needs.
- Risk Mitigation: Help businesses mitigate legal risks, protect intellectual property rights, and ensure business continuity through proactive legal counsel and strategic legal planning.

Requirements to Start:
- Legal Expertise: Build a team of experienced attorneys, legal consultants, and paralegals specializing in corporate law, contract negotiation, trademark registration, and employment law compliance.
- Client Collaboration: Conduct legal audits, business consultations, and compliance assessments to identify legal vulnerabilities, address client concerns, and develop tailored legal strategies.
- Legal Technology: Implement legal practice management software, document automation tools, and secure client portals to streamline legal workflows, document management, and client communications.

Challenges:
- Client Education: Educate startups and small businesses on legal implications, contractual obligations, and regulatory requirements to foster informed decision-making and proactive legal compliance.
- Client Acquisition: Establish trust, credibility, and long-term client relationships through thought leadership content, industry networking, and referrals within the startup and small business community.
- Legal Innovation: Embrace legal tech advancements, AI-driven legal research, and digital transformation to enhance legal service delivery, efficiency, and client satisfaction.

Scalability Opportunities:
- Service Expansion: Expand legal services to include mergers and acquisitions, corporate restructuring, international business law, and dispute resolution to meet client growth and expansion needs.
- Industry Partnerships: Collaborate with accelerators, incubators, and venture capital firms to provide legal support, due diligence services, and startup ecosystem networking opportunities.

- Virtual Legal Services: Offer virtual legal consultations, online legal document reviews, and subscription-based legal services to expand market reach, improve accessibility, and cater to remote clients.

Roadmap:
1. Market Analysis: Identify legal trends, regulatory changes, and industry challenges impacting startups and small businesses through market research, industry reports, and legal sector analysis.
2. Service Offerings: Develop service packages, pricing models, and retainer agreements tailored to startup budgets, scalability objectives, and legal advisory needs.
3. Client Engagement: Build client relationships through initial consultations, legal workshops, and ongoing legal education to empower startups with legal knowledge and strategic guidance.
4. Marketing Strategy: Implement targeted marketing campaigns, content marketing initiatives, and SEO optimization to attract startup clients, demonstrate legal expertise, and differentiate services in the competitive legal consulting market.

Further Resources:
- Legal Consulting Best Practices and Case Studies
- Tools and Technologies for Legal Practice Management

33. Strategic Planning and Advisory Services

Description: Offer strategic planning and advisory services to businesses, providing comprehensive strategic analysis, business planning, market positioning, and growth strategy development.

Marketing Insights and Opportunities:
- Business Optimization: Assist businesses in defining strategic goals, identifying growth opportunities, and developing actionable plans to enhance operational efficiency and drive sustainable growth.
- Market Differentiation: Position services as essential for competitive advantage, market expansion, and long-term business success through strategic foresight, market intelligence, and scenario planning.
- Industry Expertise: Specialize in industries such as finance, healthcare, technology, and manufacturing to offer industry-specific insights, strategic recommendations, and operational excellence.

Requirements to Start:
- Strategic Expertise: Build a team of strategic consultants, business analysts, and industry specialists with expertise in strategic planning methodologies, market research, and competitive analysis.
- Client Assessment: Conduct SWOT analysis, business diagnostics, and stakeholder consultations to assess client needs, strategic objectives, and organizational readiness for strategic planning initiatives.
- Technology Integration: Implement strategic planning software, data analytics tools, and performance management dashboards to facilitate strategic decision-making, monitor KPIs, and measure business outcomes.

Challenges:
- Client Alignment: Align strategic planning initiatives with client expectations, organizational culture, and leadership vision to ensure stakeholder buy-in and commitment to implementation.
- Complexity Management: Navigate organizational complexities, change management challenges, and strategic execution hurdles to achieve seamless integration of strategic plans and operational tactics.
- Continuous Improvement: Adapt to evolving market dynamics, industry disruptions, and competitive pressures by refining strategic frameworks, updating business models, and optimizing growth strategies.

Scalability Opportunities:
- Service Expansion: Expand advisory services to include digital transformation strategies, innovation management, and strategic partnership development to support client digitalization efforts and industry competitiveness.
- Global Strategy: Develop international market entry strategies, geographic expansion plans, and cross-border business development initiatives to capitalize on global growth opportunities and client diversification.
- Executive Coaching: Offer leadership development programs, executive coaching sessions, and management training workshops to enhance organizational leadership capabilities, strategic agility, and decision-making effectiveness.

Roadmap:
1. Market Analysis: Conduct industry analysis, competitor benchmarking, and client needs assessments to identify strategic planning gaps, growth potential, and market differentiation opportunities.
2. Service Offerings: Develop customized strategic planning frameworks, implementation roadmaps, and milestone tracking mechanisms aligned with client business objectives, industry benchmarks, and strategic priorities.
3. Client Engagement: Foster collaborative partnerships, client workshops, and strategic planning retreats to facilitate stakeholder alignment, decision consensus, and commitment to strategic goals.
4. Marketing Strategy: Launch targeted marketing campaigns, thought leadership content, and industry thought leadership initiatives to position services as industry experts, attract prospective clients, and expand market reach.

Further Resources:
- Strategic Planning Best Practices and Success Stories
- Tools and Techniques for Strategic Management and Business Planning

34. IT Support and Managed Services

Description: Provide IT support and managed services to businesses, offering proactive IT maintenance, helpdesk support, network security, cloud computing solutions, and technology infrastructure management.

Marketing Insights and Opportunities:
- Digital Transformation: Assist businesses in adopting digital technologies, improving IT efficiency, and enhancing cyber security posture through managed IT services and proactive IT support.
- Service Customization: Offer customizable IT service packages, remote monitoring solutions, and IT infrastructure management tailored to client scalability, compliance, and operational needs.
- Industry Compliance: Ensure regulatory compliance, data protection, and IT governance standards through proactive cyber security measures, risk assessments, and IT policy enforcement.

Requirements to Start:
- IT Expertise: Build a team of certified IT professionals, network engineers, cyber security specialists, and cloud architects with expertise in IT service delivery, technology integration, and client support.
- Service Infrastructure: Invest in IT service management software, remote monitoring tools, cyber security solutions, and cloud-based platforms to streamline service delivery, incident management, and client communications.
- Client Collaboration: Conduct IT assessments, infrastructure audits, and business continuity planning sessions to assess client IT needs, identify vulnerabilities, and recommend tailored IT solutions.

Challenges:
- Technology Complexity: Manage evolving technology landscapes, software updates, and cyber security threats to ensure operational continuity, data integrity, and client trust in IT service delivery.
- Service Scalability: Scale IT suppo
rt capabilities, service desk operations, and managed services offerings to accommodate client growth, technology upgrades, and digital transformation initiatives.
- Client Communication: Establish clear communication channels, service level agreements (SLAs), and incident response protocols to foster proactive client engagement, issue resolution, and service satisfaction.

Scalability Opportunities:
- Service Expansion: Expand managed IT services to include disaster recovery planning, IT consulting, virtual CIO services, and cyber security awareness training to address client cybersecurity readiness and compliance needs.
- Cloud Migration: Offer cloud migration services, hybrid cloud solutions, and IT infrastructure optimization strategies to support client digital transformation goals, scalability requirements, and cost efficiencies.
- Industry Partnerships: Collaborate with technology vendors, cyber security firms, and cloud service providers to enhance service offerings, access emerging technologies, and deliver integrated IT solutions to clients.

Roadmap:

1. Market Analysis: Identify IT service trends, cyber security threats, and client IT infrastructure needs through industry research, client surveys, and technology sector analysis.
2. Service Portfolio: Develop comprehensive IT service packages, pricing models, and service-level agreements (SLAs) aligned with client IT budgets, compliance requirements, and business continuity objectives.
3. Client Acquisition: Implement targeted marketing campaigns, client referrals, and industry networking initiatives to attract businesses seeking IT support, managed services, and cybersecurity solutions.
4. Service Excellence: Monitor service performance metrics, client feedback, and IT service delivery benchmarks to ensure service quality, client satisfaction, and continuous improvement in IT support and managed services.

Further Resources:
- IT Support Best Practices and Case Studies
- Tools and Technologies for Managed IT Services and Cybersecurity

Health and Wellness Business Overview

The health and wellness industry is rapidly growing, driven by increasing consumer awareness of personal health, fitness trends, and holistic well-being. Businesses in this sector focus on providing personalized solutions, leveraging technology, and addressing mental, physical, and nutritional aspects of wellness.

35. Personalized Nutrition Counseling

Description: Offer personalized nutrition counseling services to individuals, providing dietary assessments, meal planning, nutritional advice, and lifestyle coaching tailored to health goals and dietary preferences.

Marketing Insights and Opportunities:
- Holistic Wellness: Address the growing demand for personalized nutrition plans, dietary supplements, and wellness programs that promote overall health, weight management, and nutritional balance.
- Target Demographics: Specialize in nutrition counseling for specific demographics such as athletes, seniors, pregnant women, and individuals with dietary restrictions or health conditions to deliver targeted nutrition solutions.
- Technology Integration: Utilize nutrition tracking apps, meal planning software, and telehealth platforms to enhance client engagement, monitor progress, and provide virtual nutrition consultations.

Requirements to Start:
- Nutrition Expertise: Build a team of registered dietitians, nutritionists, and wellness coaches with expertise in nutritional counseling, dietary analysis, and behavior change techniques.
- Client Assessment: Conduct comprehensive health assessments, dietary intake evaluations, and personalized nutrition consultations to customize nutrition plans based on individual health goals and nutritional needs.
- Health and Safety Standards: Adhere to nutrition guidelines, dietary recommendations, and regulatory compliance standards to ensure client safety, ethical practice, and nutritional counseling effectiveness.

Challenges:
- Client Compliance: Address client adherence to nutrition plans, dietary recommendations, and lifestyle modifications through motivational coaching, behavioral psychology strategies, and ongoing support.
- Nutritional Diversity: Cater to diverse dietary preferences, cultural backgrounds, and nutritional requirements to provide inclusive nutrition counseling services that resonate with diverse client demographics.
- Health Education: Educate clients on nutritional principles, food labeling, dietary supplements, and sustainable eating habits to empower informed decision-making and promote long-term dietary changes.

Scalability Opportunities:
- Service Expansion: Expand nutrition counseling services to include corporate wellness programs, group workshops, online nutrition courses, and nutritional seminars to reach broader audiences and scale business growth.
- Digital Health Solutions: Develop AI-driven nutrition apps, personalized meal planning algorithms, and virtual nutrition coaching platforms to enhance service delivery, client engagement, and scalability in remote and global markets.
- Collaborative Partnerships: Partner with fitness centers, healthcare providers, wellness brands, and food manufacturers to offer integrated wellness solutions, nutritional products, and community health initiatives.

Roadmap:
1. Market Analysis: Identify nutrition trends, dietary preferences, and health challenges through consumer research, industry reports, and nutrition market analysis.
2. Service Differentiation: Develop customized nutrition programs, subscription-based services, and wellness packages tailored to client health goals, dietary preferences, and nutritional needs.
3. Client Acquisition: Implement targeted marketing strategies, nutrition workshops, and online content marketing campaigns to attract individuals seeking personalized nutrition counseling and wellness solutions.
4. Continuous Improvement: Monitor client progress, nutrition outcomes, and client feedback to refine nutrition counseling strategies, optimize service delivery, and enhance client satisfaction.

Further Resources:
- Nutrition Counseling Best Practices and Case Studies
- Tools and Technologies for Personalized Nutrition and Wellness

36. Mental Health and Wellness Apps

Description: Develop and provide mental health and wellness apps offering meditation guides, stress management techniques, mindfulness exercises, and cognitive-behavioral therapy (CBT) tools for mental well-being.

Marketing Insights and Opportunities:
- Digital Health Adoption: Address rising demand for mental health apps, online therapy platforms, and virtual support groups that promote emotional wellness, stress reduction, and mental resilience.
- Target Audience: Cater to specific demographics such as students, professionals, caregivers, and individuals experiencing anxiety, depression, or chronic stress to provide accessible mental health support.
- User Engagement: Enhance app usability, user interface (UI) design, and interactive features like mood trackers, journaling prompts, and personalized wellness plans to increase user engagement and retention.

Requirements to Start:

- Health Tech Expertise: Build a team of app developers, UX/UI designers, mental health professionals, and data privacy experts with experience in digital health solutions, app development, and mental health counseling.
- App Development: Utilize mobile app development platforms, agile development methodologies, and secure cloud infrastructure to create scalable mental health apps that comply with health data privacy regulations.
- Clinical Validation: Collaborate with mental health experts, psychologists, and behavioral scientists to validate app content, therapeutic interventions, and evidence-based mental health practices for app users.

Challenges:
- App Accessibility: Ensure app accessibility, inclusivity, and user-friendly design features for individuals with disabilities, language barriers, and diverse mental health needs to foster equal access to mental health resources.
- Content Regulation: Navigate app store guidelines, mental health app regulations, and data protection laws to ensure app compliance, secure data handling, and ethical use of user health information.
- User Trust: Build user trust, app credibility, and brand reputation through transparent app disclosures, user testimonials, and mental health community partnerships that endorse app effectiveness and user satisfaction.

Scalability Opportunities:
- Global Reach: Expand app availability, language localization, and cultural adaptation to reach international markets, diverse demographics, and underserved communities seeking accessible mental health support.
- Technology Integration: Integrate AI-driven chatbots, virtual therapists, sentiment analysis tools, and machine learning algorithms to enhance app user experience, personalize mental health interventions, and improve treatment outcomes.
- Partnership Collaboration: Forge partnerships with healthcare providers, mental health organizations, academic institutions, and corporate wellness programs to promote app adoption, referral networks, and community mental health initiatives.

Roadmap:
1. Market Research: Identify mental health app trends, user preferences, and digital health market opportunities through user surveys, app analytics, and mental health industry reports.
2. App Development: Design app prototypes, user interface wireframes, and interactive features based on user feedback, mental health research insights, and clinical expertise to ensure app usability and engagement.
3. User Acquisition: Implement app store optimization (ASO), digital marketing campaigns, and social media outreach strategies to attract app downloads, increase user engagement, and drive app adoption among target demographics.
4. App Maintenance: Monitor app performance metrics, user retention rates, and app store reviews to address user feedback, app updates, and continuous improvement in app functionality, content relevance, and user satisfaction.

Further Resources:
- Mental Health App Development Best Practices and Case Studies
- Tools and Technologies for Digital Mental Health Solutions

37. Fitness Subscription Boxes

Description: Curate and deliver fitness subscription boxes containing workout gear, fitness apparel, nutritional supplements, and wellness products tailored to fitness enthusiasts' preferences and health goals.

Marketing Insights and Opportunities:
- Fitness Lifestyle: Tap into the growing demand for fitness subscription boxes, athleisure wear, and wellness products that support active lifestyles, fitness goals, and holistic wellness practices.
- Seasonal Trends: Offer seasonal fitness box themes, workout challenges, and wellness incentives that align with fitness trends, seasonal activities, and consumer preferences for health-focused products.
- Brand Partnerships: Collaborate with fitness influencers, wellness brands, and nutrition experts to feature exclusive products, promotional offers, and subscription box incentives that enhance customer value and brand loyalty.

Requirements to Start:
- Supply Chain Management: Source fitness products, nutritional supplements, and wellness items from reputable suppliers, fitness brands, and health product manufacturers to ensure product quality, variety, and customer satisfaction.
- Subscription Box Curation: Customize fitness box contents, product assortments, and subscription pricing tiers based on customer feedback, market research insights, and seasonal fitness trends to meet subscriber expectations.
- Logistics and Fulfillment: Establish logistics partnerships, order fulfillment services, and shipping solutions to manage inventory, handle customer orders, and deliver fitness subscription boxes efficiently to subscribers.

Challenges:
- Customer Retention: Enhance subscription box value, product personalization, and customer engagement through loyalty rewards, subscription perks, and customer feedback loops that foster long-term subscriber relationships.
- Product Differentiation: Differentiate subscription box offerings, brand exclusives, and limited edition launches to attract new subscribers, retain existing customers, and increase subscription box sales in a competitive fitness market.
- Customer Experience: Optimize website usability, subscription management tools, and customer support services to streamline subscriber on boarding, address customer inquiries, and resolve subscription-related issues promptly.

Scalability Opportunities:
- Subscription Growth: Expand subscription box offerings to include themed fitness challenges, wellness programs, and lifestyle enhancements that appeal to diverse fitness interests, demographic segments, and seasonal fitness goals.
- Brand Expansion: Launch branded merchandise, fitness collaborations, and co-branded partnerships with fitness influencers, health experts, and wellness brands to extend product reach, enhance brand visibility, and attract new subscription box subscribers.

- E-commerce Innovation: Integrate AI-driven product recommendations, subscription customization tools, and predictive analytics to optimize subscriber retention, increase average order value, and enhance customer lifetime value (CLV).

Roadmap:
1. Market Analysis: Identify fitness trends, subscriber preferences, and competitive landscape analysis through consumer surveys, market research reports, and fitness industry insights.
2. Product Curation: Curate fitness box themes, product assortments, and subscription box variants based on seasonal fitness trends, customer feedback, and market demand for health and wellness products.
3. Customer Acquisition: Implement digital marketing campaigns, influencer partnerships, and social media promotions to attract fitness enthusiasts, health-conscious consumers, and lifestyle influencers interested in fitness subscription box offerings.
4. Operational Excellence: Optimize supply chain logistics, inventory management, and customer fulfillment.

38. Telemedicine Services

Description: Provide telemedicine services offering virtual doctor consultations, remote medical diagnostics, telehealth appointments, and digital prescriptions to patients seeking convenient healthcare access.

Marketing Insights and Opportunities:
- Digital Healthcare: Meet growing demand for telemedicine services, online doctor visits, and virtual healthcare solutions that improve patient access, medical care quality, and healthcare convenience.
- Patient Engagement: Enhance patient engagement, medical adherence, and chronic disease management through telehealth platforms, mobile health apps, and remote patient monitoring technologies.
- Healthcare Accessibility: Bridge healthcare gaps, rural healthcare disparities, and underserved communities' healthcare access challenges through telemedicine innovations and virtual healthcare delivery models.

Requirements to Start:
- Medical Expertise: Build a team of licensed physicians, healthcare providers, and medical specialists with telemedicine training, virtual care experience, and regulatory compliance knowledge.
- Technology Integration: Implement telehealth software, secure video conferencing tools, electronic health record (EHR) systems, and patient portal platforms to facilitate telemedicine consultations, medical data sharing, and telehealth interoperability.
- Regulatory Compliance: Ensure HIPAA compliance, telemedicine licensure, and healthcare data security protocols to safeguard patient confidentiality, medical records, and telehealth service delivery.

Challenges:

- Digital Divide: Address technology barriers, internet connectivity issues, and digital literacy disparities among patient populations to ensure equitable telemedicine access and healthcare delivery outcomes.
- Medical Liability: Navigate telemedicine malpractice risks, telehealth insurance coverage, and legal considerations to mitigate liability exposure, patient safety concerns, and healthcare liability insurance requirements.
- Healthcare Integration: Foster healthcare provider collaboration, multidisciplinary care coordination, and healthcare system integration to enhance telemedicine adoption, medical outcomes, and patient care continuity.

Scalability Opportunities:
- Specialty Services: Expand telemedicine specialties, virtual healthcare specialties, and telehealth consultations to include mental health, Teletherapy, dermatology, and chronic disease management services.
- Remote Monitoring: Integrate remote patient monitoring devices, wearable health technology, and AI-driven health analytics to support telehealth diagnostics, medical decision- making, and personalized patient care plans.
- Global Health Initiatives: Partner with international healthcare organizations, telemedicine startups, and global health agencies to promote telemedicine adoption, cross-border telehealth initiatives, and telemedicine best practices.

Roadmap:
1. Market Analysis: Identify telemedicine trends, patient preferences, and telehealth adoption rates through healthcare market research, patient surveys, and telemedicine industry analysis.
2. Service Expansion: Develop telemedicine service offerings, virtual care packages, and subscription-based telehealth models tailored to patient needs, medical specialties, and healthcare provider telemedicine capabilities.
3. Patient Engagement: Launch telemedicine marketing campaigns, patient education resources, and telehealth promotional events to increase telemedicine awareness, patient enrollment, and healthcare provider telehealth referrals.
4. Telehealth Technology: Invest in telehealth infrastructure upgrades, telemedicine software enhancements, and telehealth innovation projects to improve telemedicine usability, medical outcomes, and patient satisfaction.

Further Resources:
- Telemedicine Best Practices and Case Studies
- Tools and Technologies for Telehealth and Virtual Care

39. Mobile Fitness Training

Description: Offer mobile fitness training services, virtual workout sessions, personalized fitness plans, and online fitness coaching for individuals seeking flexible fitness solutions.

Marketing Insights and Opportunities:

- On-Demand Fitness: Cater to demand for mobile fitness apps, virtual personal training, and remote fitness coaching services that promote fitness accessibility, workout flexibility, and exercise convenience.
- Fitness Technology: Utilize fitness tracking apps, wearable fitness devices, and virtual workout platforms to deliver interactive fitness sessions, real-time performance tracking, and fitness motivation tools.
- Personalized Training: Customize fitness plans, exercise routines, and workout schedules based on client fitness goals, fitness assessments, and virtual fitness consultations.

Requirements to Start:
- Fitness Expertise: Build a team of certified fitness trainers, personal coaches, and fitness instructors with expertise in virtual fitness training, exercise physiology, and online fitness program design.
- Mobile Fitness Apps: Develop mobile fitness apps, virtual training platforms, and fitness tracking tools to facilitate virtual fitness assessments, workout scheduling, and client progress monitoring.
- Client Engagement: Conduct virtual fitness evaluations, goal-setting sessions, and fitness consultations to assess client fitness levels, determine workout preferences, and tailor personalized fitness training programs.

Challenges:
- Virtual Fitness Instruction: Adapt virtual fitness instruction techniques, coaching styles, and client motivation strategies to ensure effective communication, workout adherence, and fitness coaching effectiveness in virtual fitness environments.
- Fitness Accountability: Implement fitness accountability measures, progress tracking tools, and performance metrics to monitor client fitness goals, measure workout outcomes, and promote fitness program adherence.
- Fitness Technology: Navigate mobile app integration challenges, wearable fitness device compatibility, and fitness app usability issues to optimize virtual fitness training, enhance client engagement, and improve fitness program efficacy.

Scalability Opportunities:
- Fitness Specializations: Expand mobile fitness services to include yoga classes, HIIT workouts, strength training programs, and fitness challenges that appeal to diverse fitness interests, client demographics, and virtual fitness training preferences.
- Corporate Wellness: Partner with corporate wellness programs, fitness brands, and employee wellness initiatives to offer virtual fitness workshops, team-building exercises, and workplace fitness challenges to improve workforce health and productivity.
- Global Fitness Reach: Launch international fitness training programs, multilingual fitness coaching services, and virtual fitness memberships to extend fitness program accessibility, global fitness community engagement, and virtual fitness training reach.

Roadmap:
1. Market Research: Identify fitness app trends, virtual fitness training preferences, and mobile fitness app adoption rates through consumer surveys, fitness industry reports, and fitness technology market analysis.

2. Service Differentiation: Develop personalized fitness plans, virtual fitness training packages, and online coaching subscriptions tailored to client fitness goals, workout preferences, and fitness program customization needs.
3. Client Acquisition: Implement digital marketing strategies, social media campaigns, and influencer partnerships to promote mobile fitness apps, attract fitness enthusiasts, and increase virtual fitness training program enrollment.
4. Fitness Technology Innovation: Invest in fitness app upgrades, virtual workout platform enhancements, and wearable fitness technology advancements to enhance mobile fitness app functionality, user experience, and fitness program effectiveness.

Further Resources:
- Mobile Fitness Training Best Practices and Case Studies
- Tools and Technologies for Virtual Fitness and Mobile Training

40. Meditation and Mindfulness Classes

Description: Offer meditation and mindfulness classes, virtual mindfulness workshops, guided meditation sessions, and mindfulness-based stress reduction programs for mental well-being.

Marketing Insights and Opportunities:
- Mindfulness Trends: Address rising demand for meditation apps, online mindfulness courses, and virtual meditation classes that promote stress relief, relaxation techniques, and mental health benefits.
- Holistic Wellness: Provide mindfulness-based therapies, meditation practices, and mindfulness training programs that support mental resilience, emotional balance, and overall well-being.
- Mindfulness Education: Educate individuals on mindfulness techniques, mindfulness meditation benefits, and mindfulness exercises to enhance self-awareness, mindfulness practice integration, and mindfulness lifestyle adoption.

Requirements to Start:
- Mindfulness Expertise: Build a team of certified mindfulness instructors, meditation teachers, and mental health professionals with expertise in mindfulness-based stress reduction (MBSR), mindfulness meditation techniques, and virtual mindfulness training.
- Virtual Mindfulness Platforms: Develop virtual mindfulness platforms, meditation apps, and online meditation courses to facilitate guided meditation sessions, mindfulness training workshops, and virtual mindfulness coaching services.
- Client Engagement: Conduct mindfulness assessments, meditation consultations, and personalized mindfulness sessions to assess client mindfulness needs, establish mindfulness goals, and customize mindfulness practices.

Challenges:
- Virtual Mindfulness Instruction: Adapt virtual mindfulness teaching methods, guided meditation styles, and mindfulness coaching techniques to ensure effective mindfulness communication, meditation instruction, and client mindfulness practice engagement in virtual mindfulness environments.

- Mindfulness Accountability: Implement mindfulness practice accountability measures, mindfulness progress tracking tools, and mindfulness practice feedback mechanisms to monitor client mindfulness goals, measure mindfulness outcomes, and promote mindfulness practice adherence.
- Mindfulness Technology: Navigate virtual mindfulness platform integration challenges, mindfulness app compatibility issues, and mindfulness app usability concerns to optimize virtual mindfulness training, enhance client engagement, and improve mindfulness program effectiveness.

Scalability Opportunities:
- Mindfulness Specializations: Expand mindfulness services to include mindfulness-based cognitive therapy (MBCT), mindfulness meditation retreats, and corporate mindfulness training programs that cater to diverse mindfulness interests, client demographics, and virtual mindfulness practice preferences.
- Educational Partnerships: Partner with educational institutions, corporate wellness programs, and mindfulness research organizations to offer mindfulness workshops, mindfulness seminars, and mindfulness-based wellness initiatives that promote mindfulness education, mindfulness lifestyle adoption, and mindfulness community engagement.
- Global Mindfulness Reach: Launch international mindfulness training programs, multilingual mindfulness coaching services, and virtual mindfulness memberships to extend mindfulness program accessibility, global mindfulness community engagement, and virtual mindfulness training reach.

Roadmap:
1. Market Research: Identify mindfulness app trends, virtual mindfulness training preferences, and online mindfulness course adoption rates through mindfulness consumer surveys, mindfulness industry reports, and mindfulness technology market analysis.
2. Service Differentiation: Develop personalized mindfulness programs, virtual mindfulness training packages, and online mindfulness coaching subscriptions tailored to client mindfulness goals, mindfulness practice preferences, and mindfulness program customization needs.
3. Client Acquisition: Implement digital mindfulness marketing strategies, mindfulness social media campaigns, and mindfulness influencer partnerships to promote mindfulness apps, attract mindfulness enthusiasts, and increase virtual mindfulness training program enrollment.

Food and Beverage Business Overview

The food and beverage industry encompasses a diverse range of businesses, from restaurants and cafes to specialty food services and subscription-based culinary experiences. This sector thrives on culinary innovation, consumer dining preferences, and evolving food trends that cater to diverse tastes, dietary preferences, and dining experiences.

41. Plant-Based Fast Food Chain

Description: Establish a plant-based fast food chain offering vegan burgers, plant-based sandwiches, vegetarian wraps, and eco-friendly fast food options that appeal to health-conscious consumers and eco-friendly dining preferences.

Marketing Insights and Opportunities:
- Plant-Based Cuisine: Meet the growing demand for plant-based diets, vegan fast food options, and sustainable food choices that promote environmental sustainability, animal welfare, and healthy eating habits.
- Health Consciousness: Position plant-based fast food offerings as nutritious alternatives, vegan meal solutions, and meatless options that cater to vegan consumers, vegetarian diets, and plant-based lifestyle preferences.
- Eco-Friendly Branding: Emphasize eco-friendly packaging, sustainable sourcing practices, and organic ingredients to differentiate plant-based fast food chains, promote sustainable dining choices, and attract environmentally conscious consumers.

Requirements to Start:
- Culinary Expertise: Recruit culinary chefs, vegan chefs, and plant-based food specialists with expertise in vegan cooking techniques, plant-based recipe development, and sustainable food preparation methods.
- Menu Development: Design plant-based fast food menus, vegan meal combos, and vegetarian specials that showcase plant-based ingredients, vegan substitutes, and organic produce to appeal to health-conscious diners.
- Restaurant Operations: Establish fast food kitchen operations, food safety protocols, and eco-friendly restaurant practices to ensure vegan menu compliance, sustainable dining practices, and customer satisfaction.

Challenges:
- Consumer Education: Educate consumers on plant-based diets, vegan nutrition, and health benefits of plant-based eating to promote vegan food choices, vegetarian meal options, and plant-based lifestyle adoption among diverse demographics.
- Ingredient Sourcing: Source sustainable ingredients, plant-based proteins, and vegan substitutes from ethical suppliers, organic farmers, and eco-friendly food vendors to support vegan menu offerings, vegetarian food options, and sustainable food sourcing practices.

- Competitive Market: Navigate vegan fast food competition, plant-based restaurant trends, and consumer dining preferences to differentiate plant-based fast food chains, attract health-conscious diners, and sustain business growth.

Scalability Opportunities:
- Franchise Expansion: Expand plant-based fast food chains, vegan restaurant franchises, and vegetarian fast food outlets to multiple locations, urban markets, and global regions that support plant-based lifestyle choices, vegan dining trends, and sustainable food consumption.
- Menu Innovation: Introduce new vegan menu items, plant-based meal specials, and seasonal vegan promotions that cater to vegan consumers, vegetarian diets, and plant-based dining preferences while promoting sustainable food choices.
- Community Engagement: Partner with environmental organizations, vegan advocacy groups, and health-conscious communities to promote vegan fast food initiatives, sustainable dining practices, and eco-friendly food partnerships.

Roadmap:
1. Market Research: Identify vegan dining trends, plant-based food preferences, and sustainable food market opportunities through consumer surveys, vegan industry reports, and plant-based food market analysis.
2. Menu Expansion: Develop plant-based fast food menus, vegan meal combos, and vegetarian specials that showcase plant-based ingredients, vegan substitutes, and organic produce to appeal to health-conscious diners.
3. Brand Promotion: Implement vegan marketing strategies, eco-friendly branding initiatives, and social media campaigns to promote plant-based fast food chains, attract vegan consumers, and increase plant-based dining engagement.
4. Sustainable Practices: Adopt eco-friendly packaging, sustainable sourcing practices, and organic ingredient sourcing to support vegan menu compliance, sustainable food choices, and environmentally friendly dining experiences.

Further Resources:
- Vegan Fast Food Best Practices and Case Studies
- Sustainable Food Sourcing and Eco-Friendly Restaurant Practices

42. Specialty Coffee Roastery

Description: Establish a specialty coffee roaster offering artisanal coffee beans, single-origin coffee blends, and specialty coffee drinks that cater to coffee connoisseurs, coffee enthusiasts, and specialty coffee lovers.

Marketing Insights and Opportunities:
- Coffee Culture: Tap into specialty coffee trends, coffee connoisseurship, and third-wave coffee movements that promote artisanal coffee roasting, single-origin coffee sourcing, and gourmet coffee brewing techniques.
- Coffee Experience: Offer coffee tastings, coffee education classes, and coffee brewing workshops to enhance coffee appreciation, coffee knowledge, and specialty coffee experiences for coffee aficionados.
- Local Sourcing: Partner with coffee farmers, fair trade cooperatives, and sustainable coffee growers to source green coffee beans, organic coffee beans, and ethically

sourced coffee varieties that support coffee sustainability, environmental conservation, and coffee farm communities.

Requirements to Start:
- Coffee Roasting Expertise: Recruit master roasters, coffee roasting specialists, and coffee flavor profile experts with expertise in coffee bean roasting, coffee bean sourcing, and artisanal coffee blending techniques.
- Roastery Operations: Establish coffee roastery operations, coffee bean roasting equipment, and coffee roasting processes to ensure specialty coffee quality, coffee freshness, and coffee flavor consistency for coffee blends.
- Coffee Quality Control: Implement coffee cupping, coffee quality control measures, and coffee tasting protocols to evaluate coffee flavor profiles, coffee aroma characteristics, and coffee brewing methods that enhance coffee bean selection, coffee roasting techniques, and coffee flavor profiles.

Challenges:
- Coffee Industry Competition: Navigate specialty coffee competition, coffee market trends, and coffee Industry challenges to differentiate specialty coffee roasteries, attract coffee aficionados, and sustain coffee business growth.
- Coffee Bean Sourcing: Source green coffee beans, organic coffee beans, and direct trade coffee varieties from coffee origins, coffee regions, and coffee farmers to ensure coffee sustainability, coffee traceability, and coffee supply chain transparency.
- Coffee Consumer Preferences: Educate consumers on coffee flavor profiles, coffee brewing methods, and coffee taste preferences to promote specialty coffee appreciation, coffee culture engagement, and coffee community involvement among coffee enthusiasts.

Scalability Opportunities:
- Coffee Roastery Expansion: Expand specialty coffee roaster operations, artisan coffee roasting facilities, and coffee bean roasting capabilities to multiple locations, urban markets, and international regions that support coffee roasting excellence, coffee industry growth, and coffee quality standards.
- Coffee Branding: Develop coffee packaging designs, coffee brand identity, and coffee marketing campaigns that resonate with coffee lovers, coffee connoisseurs, and coffee enthusiasts while promoting specialty coffee brands, coffee product differentiation, and coffee brand recognition.
- Coffee Education: Launch coffee education programs, coffee brewing workshops, and coffee tasting events to educate coffee consumers, coffee industry professionals, and coffee enthusiasts on specialty coffee roasting techniques, coffee flavor profiles, and coffee brewing innovations.

Roadmap:
1. Coffee Market Research: Identify specialty coffee trends, coffee consumer preferences, and coffee market opportunities through coffee industry reports, coffee market surveys, and coffee industry analysis.
2. Coffee Roasting Expertise: Recruit master roasters, coffee roasting specialists, and coffee flavor profile experts with expertise in coffee bean roasting, coffee bean sourcing, and artisanal coffee blending techniques.

3. **Brand Promotion:** Implement coffee marketing strategies, coffee brand positioning, and coffee promotional campaigns to promote specialty coffee roasteries, attract coffee connoisseurs, and increase specialty coffee sales.

4. **Sustainable Practices:** Adopt eco-friendly packaging, sustainable sourcing practices, and organic coffee bean sourcing to support coffee sustainability, environmental conservation, and coffee industry sustainability initiatives.

Further Resources:
- Specialty Coffee Roasting Best Practices and Case Studies
- Coffee Bean Sourcing and Sustainable Coffee Practices

43. Food and Drinks Delivery Service

Description: This business aims to provide on-demand food delivery services where customers can book deliveries from any location, including homes, shops, malls, grocery stores, restaurants, and even street vendors. The service guarantees timely delivery of food items to the client's doorstep.

Marketing Insights and Opportunities:
- Target Audience: Busy professionals, aged people, families, and individuals looking for convenience.
- Marketing Channels: Utilize digital marketing (social media, paid ads), partnerships with local businesses, and SEO for online visibility.
- Unique Selling Proposition (USP): Highlight fast and reliable delivery from any source, offering convenience and flexibility.

Requirements to Start:
- Technology Platform: Develop a robust mobile app for customers to place orders and for delivery personnel to manage tasks.
- Logistics Infrastructure: Establish a network of delivery personnel (or integrate with existing delivery services), ensure reliable transportation.
- Legal Compliance: Obtain necessary permits and licenses for food handling and delivery in your operating area.

Challenges:
- Logistics Management: Ensuring timely pickups and deliveries across diverse locations.
- Quality Control: Maintaining food quality and safety standards during transit.
- Competition: Facing competition from established food delivery services.

Scalability Opportunities:
- Expansion: Scale operations to new geographic locations.
- Diversification: Expand services to include grocery delivery or specialty food items.
- Partnerships: Collaborate with more restaurants and vendors to widen service offerings.

Roadmap:
1. Market Research: Understand customer preferences and competitor analysis.
2. Technology Development: Build and test the mobile app for seamless operations.
3. Launch and Pilot: Start with a limited rollout to refine operations and gather feedback.
4. Expansion: Scale gradually based on demand and operational efficiency.

Further Resources:
- Industry Associations: Join food delivery associations for networking and insights.
- Online Courses: Learn about food logistics and delivery management.
- Books and Guides: Read resources on starting a food delivery business.

44. Food Truck Business

Description: Establish a food truck business offering gourmet street food, mobile dining experiences, and culinary delights that cater to urban foodies, food truck festivals, and community events.

Marketing Insights and Opportunities:
- Street Food Culture: Tap into food truck trends, mobile dining popularity, and gourmet street food movements that promote food truck menus, food truck festivals, and food truck catering services.
- Food Truck Experience: Provide food truck tastings, food truck tours, and food truck events to enhance street food appreciation, food truck dining experiences, and food truck community engagement for food truck enthusiasts.
- Local Ingredients: Partner with local farmers, artisanal producers, and gourmet suppliers to source fresh ingredients, organic produce, and seasonal specialties that support food truck innovation, culinary creativity, and food truck menu diversity.

Requirements to Start:
- Culinary Expertise: Recruit food truck chefs, culinary artists, and gourmet cooks with expertise in food truck cooking, street food recipes, and mobile kitchen operations for food truck events.
- Food Truck Operations: Establish food truck business operations, mobile kitchen logistics, and food truck catering services to ensure food truck quality, mobile dining experiences, and food truck sustainability for food truck customers.
- Street Food Quality Control: Implement street food tasting panels, food truck quality assurance measures, and food truck sampling protocols to evaluate street food flavors, food truck aroma characteristics, and food truck cooking techniques that enhance food truck selection, food truck packaging, and food truck distribution.

Challenges:
- Food Truck Market Competition: Navigate food truck business competition, street food industry trends, and food truck market challenges to differentiate food truck catering services, attract mobile dining enthusiasts, and sustain food truck business growth.
- Street Food Selection Variety: Source street food styles, food truck flavor profiles, and food truck categories from food truck festivals, mobile dining events, and street food vendors to promote food truck diversity, street food brand differentiation, and food truck community involvement among food truck enthusiasts.
- Food Truck Consumer Preferences: Educate food truck customers on food truck tasting techniques, street food styles, and food truck pairings to promote mobile dining appreciation, street food culture engagement, and food truck community participation in food truck catering services.

Scalability Opportunities:
- Food Truck Business Expansion: Expand food truck business offerings, street food tasting events, and food truck catering memberships to multiple regions, urban markets, and international food truck enthusiasts that support food truck business growth, street food industry expansion, and food truck market influence.
- Food Truck Branding: Develop food truck packaging designs, street food brand identity, and food truck marketing campaigns that resonate with mobile dining lovers, food truck connoisseurs, and food truck enthusiasts while promoting street food brands, food truck product differentiation, and street food brand recognition.
- Street Food Education: Launch street food education programs, food truck tasting workshops, and food truck pairing seminars to educate mobile dining consumers, street food industry professionals, and food truck enthusiasts on street food cooking techniques, food truck flavor profiles, and mobile dining innovations.

Roadmap:
1. Street Food Market Research: Identify street food trends, food truck customer preferences, and food truck market opportunities through street food industry reports, food truck market surveys, and mobile dining industry analysis.
2. Culinary Expertise: Recruit food truck chefs, culinary artists, and gourmet cooks with expertise in food truck cooking, street food recipes, and mobile kitchen operations for food truck events.
3. Brand Promotion: Implement food truck marketing strategies, food truck brand positioning, and food truck promotional campaigns to promote street food business services, attract food truck enthusiasts, and increase street food sales.
4. Sustainable Practices: Adopt eco-friendly packaging, sustainable sourcing practices, and local food truck partnerships to support street food sustainability, environmental conservation, and street food industry sustainability initiatives.

Further Resources:
- Food Truck Business Best Practices and Case Studies
- Street Food Culture and Food Truck Festival

45. Gourmet Popcorn Shop

Description: Establish a gourmet popcorn shop offering artisanal popcorn flavors, gourmet popcorn varieties, and custom popcorn creations that appeal to popcorn enthusiasts, popcorn lovers, and gourmet snack aficionados.

Marketing Insights and Opportunities:
- Popcorn Trends: Tap into gourmet popcorn trends, popcorn flavor innovation, and artisanal popcorn movements that promote popcorn shop menus, popcorn tasting events, and popcorn gift baskets.
- Popcorn Experience: Provide popcorn tastings, popcorn pairing classes, and popcorn gift sets to enhance popcorn appreciation, popcorn knowledge, and popcorn tasting experiences for gourmet popcorn lovers.
- Local Ingredients: Partner with local farmers, artisanal producers, and gourmet suppliers to source fresh ingredients, organic popcorn kernels, and seasonal popcorn

toppings that support popcorn innovation, culinary creativity, and popcorn menu diversity.

Requirements to Start:
- Culinary Expertise: Recruit popcorn chefs, culinary artists, and gourmet cooks with expertise in popcorn popping, popcorn flavoring, and popcorn seasoning for gourmet popcorn shop events.
- Popcorn Shop Operations: Establish popcorn shop business operations, gourmet popcorn logistics, and popcorn catering services to ensure gourmet popcorn quality, popcorn shop experiences, and popcorn shop sustainability for gourmet popcorn customers.
- Popcorn Quality Control: Implement popcorn tasting panels, gourmet popcorn quality assurance measures, and popcorn sampling protocols to evaluate gourmet popcorn flavors, popcorn aroma characteristics, and popcorn popping techniques that enhance popcorn selection, popcorn packaging, and popcorn distribution.

Challenges:
- Popcorn Shop Market Competition: Navigate popcorn shop business competition, gourmet popcorn industry trends, and popcorn shop market challenges to differentiate popcorn shop catering services, attract gourmet snack enthusiasts, and sustain popcorn shop business growth.
- Gourmet Popcorn Selection Variety: Source gourmet popcorn styles, popcorn flavor profiles, and gourmet popcorn categories from popcorn festivals, popcorn tasting events, and gourmet snack vendors to promote gourmet popcorn diversity, popcorn brand differentiation, and popcorn shop community involvement among popcorn enthusiasts.
- Popcorn Shop Consumer Preferences: Educate popcorn shop customers on popcorn tasting techniques, gourmet popcorn styles, and popcorn shop

Scalability Opportunities:
- Popcorn Shop Business Expansion: Expand popcorn shop offerings, gourmet popcorn tastings, and popcorn shop memberships to multiple regions, urban markets, and international gourmet snack enthusiasts that support popcorn shop business growth, gourmet popcorn industry expansion, and popcorn shop market influence.
- Popcorn Shop Branding: Develop popcorn shop packaging designs, gourmet popcorn brand identity, and popcorn shop marketing campaigns that resonate with gourmet snack lovers, popcorn connoisseurs, and popcorn enthusiasts while promoting gourmet popcorn brands, popcorn product differentiation, and popcorn shop brand recognition.
- Popcorn Shop Education: Launch popcorn shop education programs, popcorn tasting workshops, and popcorn pairing seminars to educate gourmet snack consumers, popcorn industry professionals, and popcorn enthusiasts on gourmet popcorn techniques, popcorn flavor profiles, and gourmet snack innovations.

Roadmap:
1. Popcorn Shop Market Research: Identify popcorn shop trends, gourmet popcorn preferences, and popcorn shop opportunities through popcorn shop industry reports, gourmet popcorn market surveys, and gourmet snack industry analysis.
2. Culinary Expertise: Recruit popcorn chefs, culinary artists, and gourmet cooks with expertise in popcorn popping, popcorn flavoring, and popcorn seasoning for gourmet popcorn shop events.

3. Brand Promotion: Implement popcorn shop marketing strategies, popcorn shop brand positioning, and popcorn shop promotional campaigns to promote gourmet popcorn business services, attract popcorn enthusiasts, and increase gourmet snack sales.
4. Sustainable Practices: Adopt eco-friendly packaging, sustainable sourcing practices, and local popcorn shop partnerships to support gourmet popcorn sustainability, environmental conservation, and gourmet snack industry sustainability initiatives.

Further Resources:
- Gourmet Popcorn Shop Best Practices and Case Studies
- Popcorn Flavor Innovation and Artisanal Popcorn Movements

46. Artisanal Ice Cream Production

Description: Establish an artisanal ice cream production business offering handcrafted ice cream flavors, seasonal ice cream varieties, and custom ice cream creations that appeal to ice cream enthusiasts, dessert lovers, and artisanal dessert connoisseurs.

Marketing Insights and Opportunities:
- Ice Cream Trends: Tap into artisanal ice cream trends, ice cream flavor innovation, and seasonal ice cream movements that promote ice cream menus, ice cream tasting events, and ice cream dessert parties.
- Ice Cream Experience: Provide ice cream tastings, ice cream pairing classes, and ice cream sundae bars to enhance ice cream appreciation, ice cream knowledge, and ice cream tasting experiences for artisanal ice cream lovers.
- Local Ingredients: Partner with local farmers, dairy producers, and gourmet suppliers to source fresh ingredients, organic milk, and seasonal fruits that support ice cream innovation, culinary creativity, and ice cream menu diversity.

Requirements to Start:
- Culinary Expertise: Recruit ice cream chefs, pastry artists, and dessert makers with expertise in ice cream production, ice cream flavoring, and ice cream topping for artisanal ice cream production events.
- Ice Cream Production Operations: Establish ice cream production business operations, artisanal ice cream logistics, and ice cream catering services to ensure artisanal ice cream quality, ice cream production experiences, and ice cream production sustainability for artisanal ice cream customers.
- Ice Cream Quality Control: Implement ice cream tasting panels, artisanal ice cream quality assurance measures, and ice cream sampling protocols to evaluate artisanal ice cream flavors, ice cream aroma characteristics, and ice cream production techniques that enhance ice cream selection, ice cream packaging, and ice cream distribution.

Challenges:
- Artisanal Ice Cream Market Competition: Navigate artisanal ice cream production competition, ice cream industry trends, and ice cream market challenges to differentiate artisanal ice cream production services, attract dessert enthusiasts, and sustain ice cream production business growth.
- Ice Cream Selection Variety: Source artisanal ice cream styles, ice cream flavor profiles, and artisanal ice cream categories from ice cream festivals, ice cream tasting

events, and gourmet dessert vendors to promote artisanal ice cream diversity, ice cream brand differentiation, and artisanal ice cream community involvement among ice cream enthusiasts.
- Artisanal Ice Cream Consumer Preferences: Educate artisanal ice cream customers on ice cream tasting techniques, artisanal ice cream styles, and artisanal ice cream pairings to promote artisanal ice cream appreciation, ice cream culture engagement, and artisanal ice cream community participation in artisanal ice cream catering services.

Scalability Opportunities:
- Artisanal Ice Cream Production Expansion: Expand artisanal ice cream production offerings, ice cream tasting events, and artisanal ice cream memberships to multiple regions, urban markets, and international dessert enthusiasts that support artisanal ice cream production growth, ice cream industry expansion, and artisanal ice cream market influence.
- Ice Cream Branding: Develop ice cream packaging designs, artisanal ice cream brand identity, and ice cream production marketing campaigns that resonate with dessert lovers, artisanal ice cream connoisseurs, and ice cream enthusiasts while promoting artisanal ice cream brands, ice cream product differentiation, and ice cream production brand recognition.
- Artisanal Ice Cream Education: Launch artisanal ice cream education programs, ice cream tasting workshops, and ice cream pairing seminars to educate dessert consumers, ice cream industry professionals, and ice cream enthusiasts on artisanal ice cream techniques, ice cream flavor profiles, and dessert innovations.

Roadmap:
1. Artisanal Ice Cream Market Research: Identify ice cream trends, artisanal ice cream preferences, and ice cream production opportunities through artisanal ice cream industry reports, ice cream market surveys, and dessert industry analysis.
2. Culinary Expertise: Recruit ice cream chefs, pastry artists, and dessert makers with expertise in ice cream production, ice cream flavoring, and ice cream topping for artisanal ice cream production events.
3. Brand Promotion: Implement ice cream production marketing strategies, ice cream production brand positioning, and ice cream production promotional campaigns to promote artisanal ice cream business services, attract dessert enthusiasts, and increase artisanal ice cream sales.
4. Sustainable Practices: Adopt eco-friendly packaging, sustainable sourcing practices, and local ice cream production partnerships to support artisanal ice cream sustainability, environmental conservation, and dessert industry sustainability initiatives.

Further Resources:
- Artisanal Ice Cream Production Best Practices and Case Studies
- Ice Cream Flavor Innovation and Seasonal Ice Cream Movements

Finance and Investment Business

Starting a business in finance and investment involves catering to various financial needs and goals. Whether it's facilitating peer-to-peer lending, educating teens about financial literacy, or managing impact investing funds, these ventures play crucial roles in shaping financial outcomes and fostering economic growth.

47. Peer-to-Peer Lending Platform

Description: Launch a peer-to-peer lending platform that connects borrowers seeking loans with investors looking to lend money for returns, facilitating transactions outside traditional financial institutions.

Marketing Insights and Opportunities:
- Growing Market: Tap into the expanding peer-to-peer lending market, driven by borrowers seeking alternative financing options and investors searching for higher returns.
- Tech Integration: Utilize technology to streamline loan processing, enhance user experience, and provide transparent investment opportunities.
- Risk Management: Implement robust risk assessment models to ensure borrower credibility and protect investor interests.

Requirements to Start:
- Legal Compliance: Adhere to financial regulations, obtain necessary licenses, and establish transparent terms and conditions for borrowers and lenders.
- Technology Infrastructure: Develop a secure online platform with features for loan management, investor dashboards, and automated repayment processing.
- Marketplace Development: Build a strong network of borrowers and lenders through targeted marketing, partnerships with financial institutions, and user referral programs.

Challenges:
- Regulatory Hurdles: Navigate regulatory frameworks and compliance requirements specific to peer-to-peer lending in different jurisdictions.
- Risk Mitigation: Manage default risks through thorough borrower vetting, credit scoring mechanisms, and proactive collection strategies.
- Market Competition: Differentiate from established platforms by offering unique borrower benefits, competitive interest rates, and investor protection features.

Scalability Opportunities:
- Global Expansion: Scale operations internationally by adapting to local regulations, expanding borrower outreach, and attracting diverse investor portfolios.
- Product Diversification: Introduce new lending products, such as business loans, student loans, or microfinance, to cater to evolving market demands and investor preferences.
- Technological Advancements: Innovate with blockchain technology for transparent transactions, smart contracts for automated loan agreements, and AI for risk assessment.

Roadmap:
1. Market Research: Analyze market trends, borrower preferences, and investor behavior to identify niche opportunities and competitive advantages.
2. Platform Development: Partner with tech experts to design and develop a user-friendly platform with robust security features and scalable architecture.
3. Compliance Setup: Consult legal advisors to ensure full compliance with financial regulations, data protection laws, and anti-money laundering (AML) policies.
4. Marketing Strategy: Launch targeted marketing campaigns, SEO optimization, and social media outreach to build brand awareness and attract early adopters.

Further Resources:
- Peer-to-Peer Lending Industry Reports and Case Studies
- Fintech Innovations and Regulatory Updates

48. Financial Literacy Courses for Teens

Description: Offer interactive courses and workshops designed to educate teenagers about personal finance, budgeting, saving, investing, and preparing for financial independence.

Marketing Insights and Opportunities:
- Educational Demand: Address the growing need for financial education among teens, parents, and educators seeking comprehensive curricula.
- School Partnerships: Collaborate with schools, youth organizations, and community centers to integrate financial literacy programs into educational frameworks.
- Digital Learning: Develop online courses, mobile apps, and gamified learning platforms to engage tech-savvy teens and facilitate remote learning.

Requirements to Start:
- Curriculum Development: Create age-appropriate course materials, lesson plans, and interactive resources aligned with national financial literacy standards.
- Certified Instructors: Recruit certified financial educators, guest speakers, and industry professionals to lead workshops and mentor teens.
- Parental Engagement: Involve parents in student learning through parent-teen workshops, financial planning seminars, and family-oriented activities.

Challenges:
- Education Integration: Overcome curriculum adoption barriers, funding constraints, and scheduling conflicts within school systems and extracurricular programs.
- Teen Engagement: Maintain teen interest and participation through interactive learning methods, real-life case studies, and peer group activities.
- Measuring Impact: Evaluate program effectiveness through pre-post assessments, student feedback, and longitudinal studies to demonstrate learning outcomes and societal impact.

Scalability Opportunities:
- National Outreach: Expand program reach through partnerships with educational associations, digital learning platforms, and media collaborations.

- Professional Development: Offer teacher training workshops, certification programs, and continuing education credits to empower educators in delivering financial literacy education.
- Innovative Learning Tools: Integrate AI-driven analytics, personalized learning pathways, and virtual reality simulations to enhance student engagement and knowledge retention.

Roadmap:
1. Needs Assessment: Conduct surveys, focus groups, and stakeholder interviews to assess local educational needs and identify target demographics.
2. Content Development: Collaborate with subject matter experts, curriculum specialists, and instructional designers to develop comprehensive learning modules.
3. Pilot Program: Test curriculum materials, teaching methodologies, and student assessments in pilot schools or community settings to gather feedback and refine program delivery.
4. Marketing Campaign: Launch awareness campaigns, social media promotions, and outreach events to attract students, parents, and educators to enroll in financial literacy courses.

Further Resources:
- Financial Literacy Research Reports and Educational Resources
- Youth Engagement Strategies and Educational Technology Trends

49. Impact Investing Fund

Description: Establish an impact investing fund that allocates capital to socially responsible businesses, sustainable initiatives, and community development projects aiming for both financial returns and positive societal impact.

Marketing Insights and Opportunities:
- Investor Demand: Cater to increasing investor interest in ethical investing, impact-driven portfolios, and sustainable finance solutions.
- Partnership Networks: Collaborate with NGOs, foundations, and impact-focused organizations to identify investment opportunities and leverage shared resources.
- Economic Development: Support underserved communities, environmental conservation efforts, and innovative social enterprises through strategic investment allocations.

Requirements to Start:
- Investment Strategy: Develop an impact thesis, investment criteria, and due diligence frameworks aligned with environmental, social, and governance (ESG) principles.
- Financial Expertise: Recruit experienced fund managers, financial analysts, and sustainability advisors to assess impact metrics, financial viability, and risk-return profiles of prospective investments.
- Legal Structure: Establish a fund entity, partnership agreements, and regulatory compliance procedures compliant with securities laws and fiduciary responsibilities.

Challenges:

- Impact Measurement: Define measurable impact metrics, data collection methodologies, and reporting standards to evaluate social outcomes and financial performance.
- Deal Sourcing: Identify scalable impact investment opportunities, conduct thorough market research, and engage with entrepreneurs and project developers in impact sectors.
- Stakeholder Alignment: Manage stakeholder expectations, transparency requirements, and communication strategies to build trust and credibility within the impact investing community.

Scalability Opportunities:
- Portfolio Diversification: Expand impact investment portfolios across diverse sectors, geographic regions, and emerging markets to mitigate risk and maximize positive societal outcomes.
- Sector Expertise: Develop sector-specific expertise in areas such as renewable energy, affordable housing, healthcare innovation, and inclusive finance to drive sectoral impact and investment returns.
- Impact Reporting: Implement real-time impact tracking tools, stakeholder engagement platforms, and annual impact reports to demonstrate fund performance and social value creation.

Roadmap:
1. Market Analysis: Conduct market scans, trend analysis, and competitive landscape assessments to identify impact investment opportunities and industry best practices.
2. Investment Pipeline: Cultivate relationships with impact entrepreneurs, sector experts, and ecosystem partners to source high-quality investment opportunities aligned with fund objectives.
3. Due Diligence Process: Conduct rigorous financial analysis, impact assessments, and risk evaluations to evaluate potential investments and make informed investment decisions.
4. Capital Deployment: Allocate capital, monitor portfolio performance, and provide strategic support to portfolio companies to drive growth, sustainability, and social impact outcomes.

Further Resources:
- Impact Investing Case Studies and Industry Reports
- ESG Investing Standards and Sustainable Finance Initiatives

50. Robo-Advisory Services

Description: Launch a Robo-advisory platform that uses algorithms to provide automated investment advice and portfolio management services to clients based on their financial goals and risk tolerance.

Marketing Insights and Opportunities:
- Growing Demand: Tap into the increasing demand for convenient, low-cost investment solutions among tech-savvy investors and millennials.

- Tech Integration: Utilize artificial intelligence and machine learning to optimize investment strategies, rebalance portfolios, and provide personalized financial advice.
- Financial Inclusion: Reach underserved markets and novice investors by offering accessible, user-friendly investment platforms with transparent fee structures.

Requirements to Start:
- Technology Infrastructure: Develop a secure, intuitive platform with features for account registration, risk assessment, portfolio allocation, and performance tracking.
- Regulatory Compliance: Adhere to financial regulations, obtain necessary licenses, and implement data protection measures to ensure client confidentiality and regulatory compliance.
- Customer Support: Provide responsive customer service channels, educational resources, and personalized investment insights to enhance client engagement and satisfaction.

Challenges:
- Algorithm Accuracy: Continuously refine algorithms and investment models to adapt to market fluctuations, economic trends, and changing client needs.
- Trust and Transparency: Build trust through transparent communication, clear disclosure of investment strategies, and proactive risk management practices.
- Market Competition: Differentiate from traditional financial advisors and competing robo-advisory platforms by offering unique value propositions, specialized investment products, and superior user experiences.

Scalability Opportunities:
- Global Expansion: Scale operations internationally by customizing platforms for different regulatory environments, languages, and investor preferences.
- Product Innovation: Introduce new features such as socially responsible investing options, tax-efficient portfolios, and retirement planning tools to attract diverse client demographics and enhance market competitiveness.
- Partnerships: Collaborate with financial institutions, fintech startups, and strategic partners to expand distribution channels, enhance service offerings, and leverage complementary expertise.

Roadmap:
1. Market Research: Conduct market analysis, competitor benchmarking, and client surveys to identify target demographics, market trends, and growth opportunities.
2. Technology Development: Partner with tech developers and data scientists to build and test algorithms, optimize platform performance, and ensure scalability.
3. Compliance Setup: Work with legal advisors to navigate regulatory requirements, obtain necessary licenses, and establish robust data security protocols.
4. Client Acquisition: Launch marketing campaigns, educational webinars, and referral programs to attract early adopters, build brand awareness, and grow client base.

Further Resources:
- Robo-Advisory Industry Reports and Case Studies
- AI in Financial Services and Digital Wealth Management

51. Cryptocurrency Investment Advisory

Description: Provide personalized advisory services to investors interested in navigating the complexities of cryptocurrency markets, including investment strategies, risk management, and portfolio diversification.

Marketing Insights and Opportunities:
- Emerging Market: Capitalize on the growing interest in crypto currencies among retail and institutional investors seeking high-risk, high-reward opportunities.
- Educational Demand: Offer cryptocurrency workshops, webinars, and educational resources to empower clients with knowledge about block chain technology, digital assets, and market dynamics.
- Security Concerns: Address client concerns about cyber security threats, regulatory uncertainty, and market volatility through proactive risk mitigation strategies and regulatory compliance.

Requirements to Start:
- Subject Matter Expertise: Recruit cryptocurrency analysts, block chain specialists, and investment advisors with in-depth knowledge of digital assets, decentralized finance (DeFi), and tokenomics.
- Compliance Framework: Establish compliance protocols, KYC (Know Your Customer) procedures, and AML (Anti-Money Laundering) policies to ensure regulatory adherence and client confidentiality.
- Technology Integration: Implement secure trading platforms, cryptocurrency wallets, and real-time market data analytics tools to facilitate seamless transactions and portfolio monitoring.

Challenges:
- Market Volatility: Navigate price fluctuations, market corrections, and regulatory changes that impact cryptocurrency valuations and investor sentiment.
- Risk Assessment: Conduct thorough due diligence on cryptocurrency projects, ICOs (Initial Coin Offerings), and digital exchanges to assess investment risks and opportunities.
- Client Education: Educate clients about the speculative nature of crypto currencies, risk management strategies, and long-term investment perspectives to promote informed decision-making and mitigate potential losses.

Scalability Opportunities:
- Diversified Services: Expand advisory services to include cryptocurrency custody solutions, staking-as-a-service (STAA), and yield farming strategies to cater to diverse investor preferences and risk appetites.
- Global Reach: Leverage digital platforms, multilingual support, and strategic partnerships with global exchanges to attract international clients and broaden market reach.
- Institutional Partnerships: Collaborate with fintech firms, institutional investors, and blockchain startups to develop innovative products, expand service offerings, and enhance market credibility.

Roadmap:

1. Market Analysis: Conduct market research, competitor analysis, and trend forecasting to identify niche opportunities, market entry points, and competitive advantages.
2. Advisory Framework: Develop tailored investment strategies, asset allocation models, and risk management frameworks aligned with client goals, risk tolerance, and market conditions.
3. Compliance Assurance: Engage legal advisors, compliance officers, and regulatory experts to navigate legal complexities, obtain necessary licenses, and ensure regulatory compliance.
4. Client Engagement: Launch targeted marketing campaigns, thought leadership initiatives, and client referral programs to build brand recognition, attract high-net-worth individuals, and foster long-term client relationships.

Further Resources:
- Cryptocurrency Market Research and Investment Strategies
- Block chain Technology and Digital Asset Management

52. Tax Preparation and Advisory Services

Description: Provide comprehensive tax planning, preparation, and advisory services to individuals, businesses, and organizations, ensuring compliance with tax laws and optimizing financial outcomes.

Marketing Insights and Opportunities:
- Seasonal Demand: Capitalize on peak tax season by offering timely tax filing services, tax optimization strategies, and proactive tax planning advice.
- Client Segmentation: Target specific client segments, such as small businesses, freelancers, expatriates, and high-net-worth individuals, with tailored tax solutions and personalized advisory services.
- Technology Integration: Utilize tax software, cloud-based platforms, and digital tools to streamline tax preparation processes, enhance data security, and improve client service delivery.

Requirements to Start:
- Tax Expertise: Employ certified public accountants (CPAs), tax attorneys, and enrolled agents with specialized knowledge in federal, state, and international tax regulations.
- Client Relationship Management: Implement CRM (Customer Relationship Management) systems, client portals, and communication channels to facilitate client interactions, document sharing, and service delivery.
- Compliance Assurance: Stay abreast of tax law changes, IRS (Internal Revenue Service) guidelines, and filing deadlines to ensure accurate tax reporting, penalty avoidance, and client satisfaction.

Challenges:
- Complex Tax Laws: Navigate complex tax codes, deductions, credits, and exemptions to maximize tax savings and minimize liabilities for diverse client portfolios.

- Client Expectations: Manage client expectations, confidentiality concerns, and communication challenges while providing transparent, ethical tax advice and compliance solutions.
- Competitive Landscape: Differentiate from tax preparation chains, online tax filing platforms, and DIY tax software by offering personalized advice, year-round support, and proactive tax planning services.

Scalability Opportunities:
- Service Expansion: Expand service offerings to include tax resolution services, IRS audit representation, and international tax consulting to meet evolving client needs and regulatory requirements.
- Industry Specialization: Develop industry-specific expertise in sectors such as real estate, healthcare, technology, and entertainment to address unique tax challenges and opportunities.
- Strategic Alliances: Form partnerships with financial advisors, legal professionals, and business consultants to offer integrated tax planning, wealth management, and succession planning services.

Roadmap:
1. Market Segmentation: Identify target markets, client personas, and niche service opportunities through market analysis, client referrals, and industry networking.
2. Service Development: Customize tax planning strategies, retirement planning options, and estate planning solutions based on client goals, financial profiles, and lifecycle stages.
3. Compliance Assurance: Conduct internal audits, quality control checks, and peer reviews to uphold professional standards, ethical practices, and regulatory compliance.
4. Client Education: Host tax seminars, webinars, and educational workshops to educate clients about tax law changes, filing requirements, and financial planning strategies.

Further Resources:
- Tax Preparation Best Practices and Regulatory Updates
- IRS Publications and Tax Planning Resources

Education and Training Business:

Starting a business in education and training involves providing innovative learning solutions to meet the diverse needs of learners. Whether it's launching an online language learning platform, coding bootcamps for kids, or virtual reality educational experiences, these ventures aim to enhance educational outcomes through technology-driven approaches.

53. Online Language Learning Platform

Description: Develop an online platform offering interactive language courses, tutoring services, and cultural immersion experiences to learners of all ages and proficiency levels.

Marketing Insights and Opportunities:
- Global Reach: Leverage the internet to reach a worldwide audience interested in learning languages for personal enrichment, travel, academic studies, and career advancement.
- Personalized Learning: Offer adaptive learning technologies, language proficiency assessments, and customized study plans to cater to individual learning styles and goals.
- Collaborative Learning: Facilitate language exchange programs, virtual study groups, and peer-to-peer interactions to enhance language proficiency through immersive and interactive learning experiences.

Requirements to Start:
- Curriculum Development: Create comprehensive language courses, lesson plans, and multimedia resources aligned with CEFR (Common European Framework of Reference for Languages) standards and proficiency levels.
- Technology Infrastructure: Build a user-friendly platform with features for video conferencing, interactive exercises, progress tracking, and multilingual support.
- Instructor Recruitment: Recruit qualified language instructors, native speakers, and language experts to deliver high-quality instruction, feedback, and cultural insights to learners.

Challenges:
- Competitive Landscape: Differentiate from established language learning platforms by offering unique language combinations, specialized courses (e.g., business language skills), and advanced language learning methodologies.
- User Engagement: Maintain learner motivation and participation through gamification, real-time feedback, and social learning features that promote active engagement and language fluency.
- Quality Assurance: Monitor course content, instructor performance, and user feedback to ensure instructional quality, course relevance, and continuous improvement in learning outcomes.

Scalability Opportunities:
- Expansion of Languages: Expand language offerings to include less commonly taught languages, regional dialects, and professional language skills to attract diverse learner demographics and global markets.
- Partnerships: Collaborate with educational institutions, corporate training programs, and international organizations to offer language certifications, professional development credits, and cross-cultural training solutions.
- Mobile Accessibility: Develop mobile apps, offline learning capabilities, and adaptive technologies to enhance accessibility, convenience, and flexibility for learners on-the-go.

Roadmap:
1. Market Research: Conduct market analysis, learner surveys, and competitor benchmarking to identify target markets, language learning trends, and competitive advantages.
2. Platform Development: Partner with UX designers, software developers, and language specialists to design and launch a scalable, secure, and intuitive language learning platform.
3. Content Localization: Translate course materials, cultural content, and instructional resources into multiple languages to accommodate diverse learner preferences and global audiences.
4. Marketing Strategy: Implement digital marketing campaigns, SEO optimization, and social media promotions to increase brand visibility, attract new users, and foster community engagement within the language learning community.

Further Resources:
- Language Learning Industry Reports and Educational Technology Trends
- Cross-Cultural Communication Strategies and Global Language Proficiency Assessments

54. Coding Bootcamps for Kids

Description: Offer intensive coding programs designed for children and teenagers to learn programming languages, computational thinking, and digital literacy skills in a collaborative and supportive environment.

Marketing Insights and Opportunities:
- Educational Demand: Address the growing demand for STEM education, coding proficiency, and tech skills among young learners, parents, and educators seeking future-ready competencies.
- Project-Based Learning: Emphasize hands-on coding projects, interactive workshops, and creative challenges to foster problem-solving abilities, teamwork, and innovation mindset in young participants.
- Parental Engagement: Engage parents through coding workshops, informational sessions, and progress reports to demonstrate learning outcomes, career pathways, and academic enrichment opportunities.

Requirements to Start:
- Curriculum Development: Design age-appropriate coding curricula, lesson plans, and coding exercises tailored to beginner, intermediate, and advanced coding levels.
- Instructor Qualifications: Recruit experienced coding instructors, tech mentors, and industry professionals with pedagogical expertise in coding languages (e.g., Scratch, Python, JavaScript).
- Facility Setup: Establish coding labs, equipped with computers, coding software, multimedia resources, and collaborative learning spaces conducive to experiential learning and peer interaction.

Challenges:
- Educational Integration: Align coding boot camps with school curricula, extracurricular schedules, and educational standards to complement STEM education initiatives and academic enrichment programs.
- Skill Development: Assess and monitor coding proficiency, computational thinking skills, and project-based learning outcomes to track student progress and ensure learning continuity.
- Community Building: Build a supportive learning community, parental involvement, and alumni network to foster peer-to-peer collaboration, mentorship opportunities, and lifelong learning in coding education.

Scalability Opportunities:
- Regional Expansion: Expand coding boot camps to new geographic locations, school districts, and educational institutions through franchising, partnership agreements, and remote learning options.
- Advanced Programs: Develop specialized coding tracks, Hackathons, and coding competitions to challenge advanced learners, showcase innovation projects, and attract tech-savvy participants.
- STEM Ecosystem: Collaborate with STEM educators, tech companies, and community organizations to promote coding literacy, digital skills, and career readiness among youth in underserved communities.

Roadmap:
1. Educational Needs Assessment: Conduct school partnerships, parent surveys, and teacher consultations to assess coding education gaps, learner preferences, and market demand for coding bootcamps.
2. Program Development: Design coding curricula, instructional materials, and project-based learning activities aligned with coding standards, educational objectives, and student interests.
3. Staff Training: Train coding instructors, tech mentors, and program coordinators on effective teaching strategies, classroom management, and student engagement techniques for coding bootcamps.
4. Marketing Campaign: Launch promotional campaigns, open house events, and digital marketing initiatives to raise awareness, attract student enrollments, and build brand recognition in the coding education sector.

Further Resources:
- Coding Education Research and Pedagogical Practices
- STEM Curriculum Integration and Youth Coding Initiatives

55. Virtual Reality Educational Experiences

Description: Develop immersive virtual reality (VR) educational programs and simulations that enhance learning outcomes, engagement, and retention through interactive 3D environments and virtual experiences.

Marketing Insights and Opportunities:
- Emerging Technology: Capitalize on the growing adoption of VR technology in education, training, and professional development sectors to offer innovative learning solutions and experiential learning opportunities.
- Multi-Sensory Learning: Engage learners through multisensory experiences, spatial navigation, and interactive simulations that simulate real-world scenarios, historical events, and scientific concepts.
- Educational Partnerships: Collaborate with schools, museums, cultural institutions, and corporate training programs to integrate VR educational experiences into existing curricula, field trips, and learning initiatives.

Requirements to Start:
- VR Content Development: Create immersive VR content, educational simulations, and virtual tours aligned with academic subjects, STEM disciplines, and cultural heritage sites.
- Technology Integration: Invest in VR headsets, motion-tracking sensors, haptic feedback devices, and VR development tools to create realistic environments, interactive learning modules, and user-friendly interfaces.
- Educational Pedagogy: Implement active learning strategies, assessment tools, and learning analytics to measure student engagement, cognitive development, and knowledge acquisition in VR environments.

Challenges:
- Technological Barriers: Address hardware compatibility issues, software glitches, and VR content production challenges to ensure seamless user experiences and operational reliability.
- Accessibility and Inclusivity: Design accessible VR experiences, adaptive technologies, and sensory-friendly interfaces to accommodate diverse learning styles, disabilities, and educational needs.
- Ethical Considerations: Establish guidelines for VR safety, content appropriateness, data privacy, and informed consent in educational settings to protect learner well-being and uphold ethical standards.

Scalability Opportunities:
- Customized Learning Experiences: Customize VR content, interactive simulations, and virtual field trips to meet curriculum standards, educational objectives, and learning outcomes across different grade levels and subject areas.
- Professional Development: Provide VR training modules, instructional design workshops, and teacher certification programs to empower educators with VR technology skills and pedagogical strategies.

- Global Outreach: Expand virtual learning initiatives, international partnerships, and digital collaborations to reach global audiences, multicultural learners, and remote communities with limited access to traditional educational resources.

Roadmap:
1. Needs Assessment: Conduct educational needs assessments, learner surveys, and stakeholder consultations to identify VR adoption barriers, curriculum integration challenges, and learning preferences.
2. Content Creation: Collaborate with VR developers, content creators, and subject matter experts to storyboard, script, and produce immersive educational experiences aligned with educational standards and learning objectives.
3. Pilot Testing: Test VR simulations, prototype VR environments, and user interfaces in pilot schools, educational labs, and focus groups to gather feedback, evaluate usability, and refine VR content development.
4. Deployment Strategy: Deploy VR educational experiences, training workshops, and professional development programs through strategic partnerships, online platforms, and virtual learning environments to scale impact, enhance accessibility, and promote lifelong learning.

Further Resources:
- Virtual Reality in Education Research and Case Studies
- Immersive Learning Technologies and Educational VR Applications

56. Online Tutoring Services

Description: Establish an online platform offering personalized tutoring sessions, academic support, and test preparation services across various subjects and grade levels.

Marketing Insights and Opportunities:
- Flexible Learning: Appeal to students seeking flexible scheduling, personalized learning plans, and one-on-one tutoring sessions tailored to their academic needs and learning preferences.
- Specialized Subjects: Offer tutoring services in STEM subjects, language arts, standardized test preparation, and specialized subjects to address academic challenges and promote academic success.
- Parental Engagement: Engage parents through progress reports, parent-teacher conferences, and educational resources to support student learning outcomes, academic achievement, and educational goals.

Requirements to Start:
- Tutor Recruitment: Recruit qualified tutors, subject matter experts, and certified educators with teaching credentials, academic expertise, and proficiency in virtual teaching methodologies.
- Technology Infrastructure: Invest in video conferencing software, virtual whiteboards, interactive learning tools, and secure online platforms to facilitate real-time tutoring sessions, content sharing, and student engagement.

- Quality Assurance: Implement tutor training programs, performance evaluations, and student feedback mechanisms to maintain instructional quality, learning effectiveness, and client satisfaction.

Challenges:
- Student Retention: Maintain student motivation, academic progress, and learning continuity through personalized learning strategies, adaptive tutoring techniques, and ongoing support.
- Competitive Differentiation: Differentiate from traditional tutoring centers, online learning platforms, and peer-to-peer tutoring networks by offering value-added services, personalized learning plans, and academic support resources.
- Technological Dependence: Address technical challenges, connectivity issues, and cybersecurity concerns to ensure reliable, secure, and uninterrupted online tutoring sessions for students and tutors.

Scalability Opportunities:
- Global Reach: Expand tutoring services internationally through multilingual support, cultural competency training, and strategic partnerships with educational institutions, homeschooling networks, and international student programs.
- Subject Specialization: Offer specialized tutoring programs in STEM disciplines, college admissions consulting, advanced placement courses, and specialized academic subjects to attract diverse student demographics and academic interests.
- Educational Partnerships: Collaborate with schools, universities, and community organizations to offer tutoring scholarships, academic enrichment programs, and supplemental learning opportunities for underserved student populations.

Roadmap:
1. Market Analysis: Conduct market research, student surveys, and parent feedback to identify educational needs, academic challenges, and tutoring preferences within target demographics.
2. Platform Development: Customize online tutoring platforms, virtual learning environments, and mobile applications to optimize user experience, accessibility, and educational outcomes for students, parents, and educators.
3. Tutor Training: Provide ongoing professional development, pedagogical training, and instructional resources to tutors, mentors, and academic coaches to enhance teaching effectiveness, student engagement, and learning outcomes.
4. Marketing Strategy: Launch digital marketing campaigns, social media promotions, and educational webinars to raise brand awareness, attract new students, and foster community engagement within the online tutoring marketplace.

Further Resources:
- Online Tutoring Trends and Educational Technology Innovations
- Parental Involvement in Student Academic Success and Online Learning Best Practices

57. Music Lessons and Instrument Rentals

Description: Offer music education programs, private lessons, instrument rentals, and ensemble opportunities to students of all ages and skill levels interested in learning music theory, performance techniques, and musical instrument proficiency.

Marketing Insights and Opportunities:
- Multi-sensory Learning: Engage students through interactive music lessons, group workshops, and performance opportunities that promote creativity, self-expression, and musical skill development.
- Community Engagement: Partner with local schools, community centers, and cultural institutions to offer music education programs, youth orchestras, and community concerts that showcase student talent and promote music appreciation.
- Instrument Access: Provide affordable instrument rentals, maintenance services, and instrument purchase options to support student access to high-quality musical instruments and equipment.

Requirements to Start:
- Music Faculty: Recruit qualified music instructors, professional musicians, and certified music educators with expertise in music theory, instrumental techniques, and performance coaching.
- Facility Setup: Establish music studios, practice rooms, and rehearsal spaces equipped with musical instruments, audiovisual equipment, and acoustically treated environments conducive to music learning and ensemble rehearsals.
- Curriculum Development: Design comprehensive music curricula, instructional materials, and performance repertoire that align with music education standards, student skill levels, and learning objectives.

Challenges:
- Student Recruitment: Attract new students, retain enrolments, and maintain student engagement through diverse music education offerings, promotional events, and community outreach initiatives.
- Instrument Inventory: Manage inventory, procurement, and maintenance of musical instruments, accessories, and equipment to ensure availability, quality assurance, and optimal performance for student use.
- Performance Opportunities: Coordinate music recitals, ensemble performances, and community concerts that showcase student achievements, foster artistic growth, and promote musical excellence within the local community.

Scalability Opportunities:
- Program Expansion: Expand music education programs to include specialized workshops, masterclasses, summer music camps, and interdisciplinary arts collaborations that attract diverse student demographics and promote lifelong music learning.
- Digital Learning: Develop online music lessons, virtual rehearsals, and digital platforms for music theory instruction, instrumental practice, and collaborative music-making experiences that enhance accessibility, flexibility, and global outreach.
- Community Partnerships: Form partnerships with music festivals, performing arts centers, and music industry professionals to offer guest artist residencies, mentorship programs, and career development opportunities for aspiring musicians.

Roadmap:

1. Needs Assessment: Conduct student assessments, parent surveys, and community needs analyses to identify music education gaps, programmatic priorities, and funding opportunities within the local arts and culture sector.
2. Curriculum Enhancement: Collaborate with music educators, curriculum specialists, and instructional designers to integrate music technology, digital learning tools, and interdisciplinary arts experiences into music education curricula.
3. Performance Logistics: Coordinate concert logistics, rehearsal schedules, and performance venues to facilitate student participation in music festivals, regional competitions, and community outreach events.
4. Marketing Strategy: Implement marketing campaigns, social media promotions, and outreach initiatives to promote music education programs, recruit new students, and engage community stakeholders in supporting arts education initiatives.

Further Resources:
- Music Education Research and Best Practices
- Arts Integration and Community Arts Partnerships

58. Career Skills Development Workshops

Description: Provide interactive workshops, professional development seminars, and career coaching services designed to enhance employability skills, career readiness, and workplace competencies for job seekers, professionals, and aspiring entrepreneurs.

Marketing Insights and Opportunities:
- Career Advancement: Address the demand for career skills training, job search strategies, and professional networking opportunities among individuals seeking career transitions, skill upgrades, and professional development.
- Industry Expertise: Offer industry-specific workshops, sector-specific certifications, and career pathways that align with emerging job trends, market demands, and economic opportunities within key industries.
- Corporate Partnerships: Collaborate with employers, HR departments, and workforce development agencies to deliver customized training programs, corporate workshops, and leadership development initiatives that address organizational skills gaps and workforce training needs.

Requirements to Start:
- Subject Matter Experts: Recruit experienced career coaches, industry consultants, and certified trainers with expertise in career development, job placement services, and vocational guidance.
- Curriculum Design: Develop tailored workshops, skill-building modules, and professional development resources that cover resume writing, interview preparation, networking strategies, and workplace etiquette.
- Facilitator Training: Train workshop facilitators, career advisors, and guest speakers on effective presentation techniques, adult learning principles, and interactive workshop methodologies to enhance participant engagement and learning outcomes.

Challenges:

- Skill Diversification: Address diverse participant needs, career aspirations, and skill development goals through personalized coaching sessions, skills assessments, and career planning consultations.
- Market Differentiation: Position career skills workshops, industry certifications, and professional development programs as value-added services that enhance employability, career advancement, and workplace productivity.
- Participant Engagement: Maintain participant motivation, attendance rates, and program satisfaction through ongoing feedback loops, performance evaluations, and continuous improvement initiatives in workshop design and delivery.

Scalability Opportunities:
- Specialized Training: Expand workshop offerings to include leadership development programs, executive coaching services, and industry-specific certifications that cater to niche markets, professional associations, and corporate training needs.
- E-Learning Platforms: Launch online career skills courses, virtual workshops, and digital learning modules that accommodate remote learners, global audiences, and lifelong learners seeking flexible, accessible career development solutions.
- Employer Partnerships: Form strategic alliances with corporate clients, industry associations, and workforce development agencies to develop customized training solutions, talent pipeline initiatives, and employer-sponsored career advancement programs.

Roadmap:
1. Needs Assessment: Conduct workforce surveys, skills gap analyses, and employer consultations to identify priority skills, training needs, and career development opportunities within target industries and job sectors.
2. Program Development: Design curriculum frameworks, competency-based assessments, and skill-building workshops that align with industry standards, workforce readiness benchmarks, and professional accreditation requirements.
3. Participant Outreach: Implement marketing campaigns, employer outreach initiatives, and recruitment strategies to attract job seekers, mid-career professionals, and corporate clients interested in career skills development workshops.
4. Evaluation Metrics: Track participant outcomes, program impact, and return on investment (ROI) through participant evaluations, skills assessment.

Sustainability and Green Business

Starting a business in sustainability and green initiatives involves offering innovative solutions that prioritize environmental responsibility, resource efficiency, and sustainable practices. Whether it's urban farming solutions, renewable energy consultancy, or eco-friendly packaging solutions, these ventures aim to promote ecological stewardship and address pressing environmental challenges.

59. Urban Farming Solutions

Description: Develop urban farming solutions such as rooftop gardens, vertical farming systems, and hydroponic setups to promote local food production, urban greening, and sustainable agriculture practices.

Marketing Insights and Opportunities:
- Urban Resilience: Address urban food security, community health, and environmental sustainability by promoting local food production, reducing food miles, and minimizing carbon footprint.
- Educational Outreach: Engage schools, community centers, and urban dwellers through educational workshops, urban farming tours, and hands-on gardening experiences that promote environmental awareness and food sovereignty.
- Community Partnerships: Collaborate with local governments, urban planners, and sustainability initiatives to integrate urban farming into urban development plans, green infrastructure projects, and sustainable city initiatives.

Requirements to Start:
- Site Selection: Identify suitable urban spaces, rooftops, and vacant lots for urban farming installations, ensuring access to sunlight, water supply, and community support for agricultural activities.
- Technology Integration: Invest in vertical farming technologies, hydroponic systems, and IoT sensors for efficient water management, crop monitoring, and climate control in urban farming environments.
- Crop Diversity: Grow a variety of fruits, vegetables, herbs, and medicinal plants that thrive in urban settings, addressing dietary diversity, nutritional needs, and seasonal crop production challenges.

Challenges:
- Regulatory Compliance: Navigate zoning regulations, land use policies, and urban farming ordinances to secure permits, land leases, and community support for urban agriculture initiatives.
- Resource Constraints: Manage water usage, energy consumption, and operational costs associated with urban farming infrastructure, equipment maintenance, and crop cultivation in urban environments.
- Community Engagement: Foster inclusive urban farming practices, volunteer opportunities, and stakeholder partnerships to promote social equity, community resilience, and food justice within urban communities.

Scalability Opportunities:

- Food Sovereignty: Expand urban farming networks, community-supported agriculture (CSA) programs, and farmer's markets to increase access to locally grown produce, organic foods, and sustainably sourced agricultural products.
- Green Technology: Develop smart farming solutions, renewable energy integration, and circular economy practices that optimize resource efficiency, minimize environmental impact, and enhance urban farming scalability.
- Policy Advocacy: Advocate for supportive policies, incentives, and funding opportunities for urban agriculture, sustainable food systems, and green infrastructure development at local, regional, and national levels.

Roadmap:
1. Feasibility Study: Conduct site assessments, market research, and stakeholder consultations to assess urban farming feasibility, market demand, and community interest in sustainable agriculture initiatives.
2. Project Planning: Design urban farming layouts, irrigation systems, and crop management plans that align with urban planning goals, environmental sustainability targets, and community development priorities.
3. Partnership Development: Collaborate with local farmers, urban gardeners, and food justice organizations to build partnerships, share best practices, and promote collective action on urban farming, food security, and community resilience.
4. Public Engagement: Launch educational campaigns, social media outreach, and community events to raise awareness, build support, and mobilize grassroots efforts for urban farming, environmental stewardship, and sustainable food systems.

Further Resources:
- Urban Agriculture Research and Sustainable Food Systems Initiatives
- Green Building Technologies and Urban Greening Strategies

60. Renewable Energy Consultancy

Description: Provide consultancy services in renewable energy solutions, energy efficiency audits, and sustainable energy planning to businesses, governments, and residential clients seeking to reduce carbon footprint and transition to clean energy sources.

Marketing Insights and Opportunities:
- Energy Transition: Address global climate goals, regulatory mandates, and corporate sustainability commitments by offering renewable energy solutions, carbon reduction strategies, and energy-efficient technologies.
- Sector Expertise: Specialize in solar PV systems, wind energy projects, energy storage solutions, and smart grid technologies to meet diverse energy needs, market demands, and technological advancements in renewable energy.
- Policy Compliance: Assist clients with renewable energy incentives, tax credits, and compliance with environmental regulations, energy codes, and sustainability certifications.

Requirements to Start:

- Technical Expertise: Recruit renewable energy engineers, energy analysts, and certified energy auditors with expertise in renewable energy technologies, energy modeling, and sustainable building design.
- Client Engagement: Conduct energy assessments, feasibility studies, and energy audits to identify energy-saving opportunities, cost-effective solutions, and return on investment (ROI) for renewable energy projects.
- Project Management: Coordinate project planning, permitting processes, and construction management for renewable energy installations, grid integration, and energy infrastructure upgrades.

Challenges:
- Market Competitiveness: Differentiate from energy consulting firms, engineering companies, and utility providers by offering specialized expertise, innovative solutions, and customized energy strategies tailored to client needs.
- Technology Integration: Address scalability challenges, grid reliability issues, and energy storage solutions to optimize renewable energy deployment, operational efficiency, and sustainable energy management practices.
- Client Education: Educate stakeholders, decision-makers, and community leaders on renewable energy benefits, technological advancements, and financial incentives to support informed decision-making and sustainable energy investments.

Scalability Opportunities:
- Industry Partnerships: Collaborate with renewable energy developers, technology providers, and financial institutions to expand project financing options, investment opportunities, and market penetration in emerging renewable energy markets.
- Policy Advocacy: Advocate for renewable energy policies, clean energy incentives, and regulatory reforms that support renewable energy deployment, grid modernization, and sustainable energy infrastructure development.
- International Markets: Explore global renewable energy markets, cross-border partnerships, and international projects that promote renewable energy integration, climate resilience, and sustainable development goals.

Roadmap:
1. Market Analysis: Conduct market research, industry trends analysis, and competitive benchmarking to identify renewable energy opportunities, market niches, and client demand for clean energy solutions.
2. Client Engagement: Develop customized energy solutions, project proposals, and renewable energy portfolios that align with client sustainability goals, energy efficiency targets, and financial investment criteria.
3. Project Implementation: Manage renewable energy projects, stakeholder consultations, and project delivery milestones to ensure quality assurance, regulatory compliance, and successful energy outcomes.
4. Thought Leadership: Publish industry reports, white papers, and thought leadership content on renewable energy innovations, sustainable energy practices, and industry best practices to enhance brand visibility, client trust, and market credibility.

Further Resources:
- Renewable Energy Market Reports and Industry Insights
- Clean Energy Financing Options and Green Investment Strategies

61. Eco-Friendly Packaging Solutions

Description: Develop and supply eco-friendly packaging materials, sustainable packaging designs, and biodegradable packaging solutions to businesses, e-commerce retailers, and consumer brands aiming to reduce environmental impact and promote sustainable consumption practices.

Marketing Insights and Opportunities:
- Circular Economy: Support circular packaging initiatives, zero-waste goals, and sustainable packaging innovations that minimize plastic pollution, promote recycling, and improve product lifecycle management.
- Consumer Preference: Respond to consumer demand for eco-friendly products, green packaging options, and environmentally responsible brands that prioritize sustainability, ethical sourcing, and corporate social responsibility.
- Brand Differentiation: Partner with eco-conscious brands, green startups, and sustainable fashion labels to offer customized packaging solutions, brand storytelling, and eco-labeling strategies that resonate with environmentally aware consumers.

Requirements to Start:
- Material Innovation: Source renewable materials, bio plastics, and compostable packaging alternatives that meet eco-certifications, regulatory standards, and sustainable packaging guidelines (e.g., ASTM D6400, EN 13432).
- Design Expertise: Collaborate with packaging designers, graphic artists, and sustainability consultants to develop eco-friendly packaging designs, minimalist packaging solutions, and innovative packaging prototypes.
- Supply Chain Management: Establish partnerships with packaging suppliers, logistics providers, and material recyclers to ensure supply chain transparency, product traceability, and sustainable sourcing practices.

Challenges:
- Cost Efficiency: Manage production costs, material procurement expenses, and packaging design investments to offer competitive pricing, cost-effective solutions, and sustainable packaging options without compromising product quality or brand integrity.
- Regulatory Compliance: Navigate packaging regulations, environmental legislation, and packaging waste directives to comply with extended producer responsibility (EPR), packaging recovery targets, and environmental stewardship obligations.
- Consumer Education: Educate consumers, retailers, and supply chain stakeholders on eco-friendly packaging benefits, green packaging certifications, and sustainable packaging practices to foster informed decision-making and responsible packaging choices.

Scalability Opportunities:
- Market Expansion: Expand eco-friendly packaging solutions to new industries, market segments, and global markets through strategic partnerships, distribution networks, and sustainable packaging innovations.

- Product Innovation: Develop biodegradable packaging materials, reusable packaging designs, and closed-loop packaging systems that support circular economy principles, resource efficiency, and waste reduction initiatives.
- Corporate Sustainability: Partner with corporate clients, multinational brands, and industry leaders to implement sustainable packaging policies, carbon-neutral packaging strategies, and supply chain sustainability initiatives.

Roadmap:
1. Market Assessment: Conduct packaging audits, sustainability assessments, and lifecycle analysis studies to evaluate packaging impacts, environmental footprints, and sustainable packaging solutions.
2. Design Development: Collaborate with packaging engineers, material scientists, and design professionals to prototype eco-friendly packaging solutions, sustainable packaging prototypes, and green packaging innovations.
3. Supply Chain Integration: Implement sustainable sourcing practices, ethical procurement policies, and green supply chain initiatives to support circular economy principles, supply chain resilience, and sustainable packaging best practices.
4. Brand Engagement: Launch marketing campaigns, eco-labeling initiatives, and consumer engagement programs.

62. Upcycled Furniture Design

Description: Create and sell unique furniture pieces crafted from reclaimed materials such as wood, metal, and textiles, promoting sustainable practices and artistic expression in home decor.

Marketing Insights and Opportunities:
- Artistic Appeal: Target environmentally conscious consumers seeking bespoke furniture pieces, custom designs, and artisanal craftsmanship that reflect sustainability values and eco-friendly lifestyles.
- Interior Design Trends: Capitalize on up cycled furniture trends, vintage decor styles, and rustic home furnishings that appeal to eco-conscious homeowners, interior designers, and boutique retailers.
- Community Engagement: Collaborate with local artists, up cycling workshops, and community art projects to showcase sustainable design, creative reuse, and environmental stewardship through furniture restoration and up cycling.

Requirements to Start:
- Material Sourcing: Collect salvaged materials, discarded furniture pieces, and reclaimed resources from construction sites, recycling centers, and salvage yards for up cycling into new furniture designs.
- Craftsmanship: Employ skilled artisans, furniture makers, and carpenters proficient in up cycling techniques, furniture restoration, and sustainable woodworking practices to create durable, functional, and aesthetically pleasing furniture pieces.
- Product Line: Develop a diverse product line of up cycled furniture, refurbished antiques, and custom-made pieces tailored to customer preferences, interior design trends, and sustainable living standards.

Challenges:
- Supply Chain Management: Secure reliable sources of reclaimed materials, sustainable wood supplies, and eco-friendly finishes to ensure product quality, material integrity, and environmental sustainability in furniture production.
- Market Differentiation: Differentiate from mass-produced furniture brands, retail chains, and online marketplaces by offering handmade craftsmanship, personalized design consultations, and eco-conscious furniture collections that appeal to discerning consumers.
- Consumer Education: Educate consumers, interior designers, and sustainable living advocates on the benefits of up cycled furniture, environmental impact reduction, and circular economy principles that promote resource conservation and waste minimization.

Scalability Opportunities:
- Online Presence: Expand e-commerce sales channels, digital marketing campaigns, and online marketplace listings to reach global audiences, international buyers, and eco-friendly consumers interested in sustainable home furnishings.
- Collaborative Partnerships: Form partnerships with interior design firms, home decor boutiques, and sustainable living influencers to showcase up cycled furniture collections, eco-friendly lifestyle products, and sustainable design innovations.
- Circular Economy Initiatives: Implement closed-loop production models, furniture refurbishment services, and product recycling programs that promote waste reduction, material recovery, and environmental sustainability within the furniture industry.

Roadmap:
1. Design Innovation: Explore up cycling techniques, furniture design trends, and sustainable materials to create unique furniture collections, signature pieces, and custom-made designs that align with market demand and consumer preferences.
2. Brand Development: Build brand awareness, brand identity, and brand loyalty through eco-friendly branding, sustainable packaging, and transparent supply chain practices that communicate environmental values and ethical business practices.
3. Market Expansion: Launch promotional campaigns, furniture showcases, and sustainability workshops to engage target demographics, educate consumers, and cultivate community support for upcycled furniture, sustainable living, and environmental stewardship.
4. Impact Measurement: Track environmental metrics, carbon footprint reductions, and waste diversion rates to quantify the environmental benefits, social impact, and sustainable outcomes of upcycled furniture production and circular economy initiatives.

Further Resources:
- Sustainable Furniture Design Principles and Circular Economy Strategies
- Up cycling Trends in Home Decor and Environmental Sustainability

63. Water Purification Systems

Description: Provide water purification systems, filtration technologies, and clean water solutions to residential, commercial, and industrial clients seeking safe, sustainable drinking water sources.

Marketing Insights and Opportunities:
- Water Quality: Address global water scarcity, water pollution concerns, and public health risks by offering water purification systems, reverse osmosis technologies, and advanced filtration solutions that enhance water quality, taste, and safety.
- Market Demand: Tap into the growing market demand for sustainable water management solutions, water conservation technologies, and eco-friendly water purification systems that support environmental sustainability goals.
- Public Health Initiatives: Partner with healthcare facilities, educational institutions, and community organizations to promote safe drinking water practices, waterborne disease prevention, and public health awareness through water purification initiatives.

Requirements to Start:
- Technology Expertise: Partner with water treatment specialists, environmental engineers, and certified water quality experts to design, install, and maintain water purification systems, filtration equipment, and water testing services that comply with regulatory standards and industry best practices.
- Product Selection: Offer a range of water treatment solutions, point-of-use filters, and whole-house water purification systems tailored to customer needs, water quality challenges, and regional water supply issues.
- Service Integration: Provide installation services, maintenance programs, and customer support for water purification systems, UV disinfection units, and carbon filtration systems to ensure system performance, water safety, and client satisfaction.

Challenges:
- Technological Integration: Address technical challenges, system compatibility issues, and water treatment complexities associated with integrating water purification technologies, filtration processes, and disinfection methods into existing water supply infrastructures.
- Regulatory Compliance: Navigate water quality regulations, drinking water standards, and environmental permits to meet regulatory requirements, water quality criteria, and public health guidelines for safe drinking water compliance.
- Consumer Awareness: Educate consumers, business owners, and public stakeholders on water contamination risks, water treatment solutions, and preventive measures to promote water conservation, environmental stewardship, and sustainable water management practices.

Scalability Opportunities:
- Market Expansion: Expand water purification services, filtration product lines, and clean water solutions to new markets, geographic regions, and emerging economies where access to safe drinking water, water infrastructure development, and water quality improvement initiatives are priorities.
- Technology Innovation: Invest in water treatment research, innovation partnerships, and next-generation water purification technologies that improve water efficiency, reduce energy consumption, and enhance water quality standards for sustainable development goals.

- Corporate Partnerships: Collaborate with corporate clients, municipal governments, and international organizations to implement water purification projects, infrastructure investments, and public-private partnerships that promote water security, environmental sustainability, and community resilience.

Roadmap:
1. Market Analysis: Conduct water quality assessments, client surveys, and feasibility studies to identify water purification needs, market opportunities, and customer preferences for sustainable water solutions.
2. Solution Design: Customize water treatment systems, filtration technologies, and water purification strategies that align with client specifications, water quality objectives, and environmental sustainability goals.
3. Project Implementation: Manage water purification projects, regulatory approvals, and system installations for residential, commercial, and industrial clients to ensure water safety, regulatory compliance, and long-term operational performance.
4. Community Engagement: Launch educational campaigns, water conservation workshops, and public awareness initiatives to promote water stewardship, sustainable water practices, and community involvement in water purification efforts.

Further Resources:
- Water Purification Technologies and Sustainable Water Management Practices
- Global Water Crisis Solutions and Safe Drinking Water Initiatives

64. Sustainable Fashion Rental Service

Description: Launch a sustainable fashion rental platform offering clothing rentals, eco-friendly fashion options, and circular fashion solutions to promote textile reuse, reduce fashion waste, and encourage sustainable consumer habits.

Marketing Insights and Opportunities:
- Fashion Sustainability: Address fast fashion impacts, textile waste concerns, and environmental footprint reductions by offering clothing rental subscriptions, capsule wardrobes, and seasonal fashion collections that promote sustainable fashion choices.
- Consumer Behavior: Tap into the sharing economy, collaborative consumption trends, and conscious consumerism movements that prioritize fashion sustainability, ethical fashion practices, and eco-friendly clothing alternatives.
- Fashion Innovation: Partner with fashion designers, sustainable brands, and ethical fashion labels to showcase eco-friendly materials, zero-waste fashion designs, and circular economy models that promote textile recycling, garment durability, and fashion durability.

Requirements to Start:
- Fashion Curation: Curate a diverse fashion collection, designer labels, and trendy styles that appeal to fashion-forward consumers, eco-conscious shoppers, and sustainability advocates interested in sustainable fashion rental services.
- Logistics Management: Develop inventory management systems, garment tracking software, and logistics solutions for clothing pickup, dry cleaning services, and garment maintenance to ensure garment quality, cleanliness, and customer satisfaction.

- Membership Services: Offer rental subscriptions, fashion memberships, and personalized styling services that cater to customer preferences, fashion trends, and seasonal wardrobe updates for sustainable fashion choices.

Challenges:
- Supply Chain Transparency: Ensure supply chain transparency, ethical sourcing practices, and sustainable fashion certifications that verify fair trade practices, organic materials, and eco-friendly production methods in garment manufacturing.
- Fashion Access: Address wardrobe challenges, size inclusivity, and fashion accessibility barriers by offering diverse fashion options, size ranges, and clothing styles that accommodate diverse consumer needs, fashion preferences, and personal style preferences.
- Consumer Education: Educate consumers, fashion influencers, and industry stakeholders on sustainable fashion benefits, circular economy principles, and textile reuse strategies to promote fashion sustainability, clothing longevity, and eco-friendly fashion choices.

Scalability Opportunities:
- Market Expansion: Expand fashion rental services, rental subscription models, and clothing exchange programs to new markets, international audiences, and global fashion capitals that prioritize sustainable fashion trends, fashion sustainability goals, and textile recycling initiatives.
- Fashion Innovation: Collaborate with fashion tech startups, textile recycling companies, and sustainable fashion innovators to develop garment rental platforms, digital wardrobe apps, and smart fashion solutions that enhance fashion accessibility.
- Partnership Development: Form partnerships with corporate brands, fashion retailers, and eco-friendly startups to promote sustainable fashion initiatives, circular fashion practices, and collaborative fashion projects that advance environmental sustainability, textile waste reduction, and fashion industry innovation.

Roadmap:
1. Market Analysis: Conduct market research, trend analysis, and consumer surveys to identify sustainable fashion trends, rental market opportunities, and customer preferences for eco-friendly fashion choices.
2. Platform Development: Build a user-friendly website, mobile app, and online marketplace for fashion rentals, personalized styling services, and virtual fashion experiences that enhance customer engagement, fashion accessibility, and sustainable fashion impact.
3. Community Engagement: Launch marketing campaigns, social media initiatives, and fashion events to build brand awareness, promote sustainable fashion values, and foster community participation in clothing rental services, fashion sustainability, and textile recycling programs.
4. Impact Measurement: Track environmental metrics, clothing reuse rates, and fashion waste reductions to quantify the environmental benefits, social impact, and sustainable outcomes of fashion rental services, circular fashion initiatives, and sustainable fashion investments.

Further Resources:
- Sustainable Fashion Design Principles and Circular Economy Strategies
- Fashion Rental Platforms and Green Fashion Innovations

Creative Arts and Media Businesses

Starting a business in creative arts and media involves offering innovative services that cater to digital content creation, online art education, and podcast production. These ventures aim to leverage creativity, digital platforms, and media production techniques to engage audiences, educate learners, and entertain listeners in today's digital landscape.

65. Digital Content Creation Agency

Description: Establish a digital content creation agency offering services such as video production, digital marketing campaigns, social media content, and creative branding solutions for businesses seeking to enhance their online presence and engage with their target audiences effectively.

Marketing Insights and Opportunities:
- Content Diversity: Provide diverse content creation services including video production, animation, graphic design, and multimedia storytelling to cater to the visual storytelling needs of businesses across various industries.
- Digital Engagement: Utilize social media platforms, digital advertising strategies, and interactive content formats to increase audience engagement, brand awareness, and customer loyalty through creative content campaigns.
- Market Demand: Address the growing demand for digital content services, content marketing solutions, and visual storytelling strategies that enhance brand visibility, customer engagement, and online marketing effectiveness.

Requirements to Start:
- Creative Talent: Recruit skilled videographers, graphic designers, content creators, and digital marketers proficient in digital media production, creative storytelling, and multimedia content creation techniques to deliver high-quality digital content services.
- Technology Infrastructure: Invest in professional-grade cameras, video editing software, graphic design tools, and digital content creation platforms that support creative production workflows, collaborative project management, and client deliverables.
- Client Portfolio: Build a diverse client portfolio, industry partnerships, and client referrals through networking, client testimonials, and case studies showcasing successful digital content campaigns, brand collaborations, and creative marketing strategies.

Challenges:
- Competitive Landscape: Navigate competitive pressures, evolving digital trends, and industry disruptors in the digital content creation market by offering differentiated

services, innovative content solutions, and personalized client experiences that meet client objectives and business goals.
- Content Quality: Ensure content consistency, creative excellence, and brand alignment in digital content campaigns, visual storytelling projects, and multimedia productions to maintain client satisfaction, audience engagement, and brand reputation.
- Project Scalability: Manage project scalability, resource allocation, and production timelines for simultaneous client projects, content creation campaigns, and digital media initiatives that require effective project management, client communication, and team collaboration.

Scalability Opportunities:
- Service Expansion: Expand service offerings to include augmented reality (AR) experiences, virtual reality (VR) content, immersive storytelling formats, and interactive multimedia campaigns that enhance digital engagement, audience interaction, and brand storytelling capabilities.
- Industry Partnerships: Form strategic alliances with marketing agencies, creative studios, and digital platforms to collaborate on joint ventures, content co-creation projects, and integrated marketing campaigns that leverage combined expertise, industry insights, and creative resources.
- Global Reach: Utilize digital distribution channels, online platforms, and global marketplaces to reach international audiences, expand market presence, and scale digital content services across diverse geographic regions, cultural demographics, and industry sectors.

Roadmap:
1. Market Research: Conduct market analysis, client needs assessments, and competitive benchmarking to identify market opportunities, client pain points, and industry trends driving demand for digital content creation services.
2. Service Differentiation: Develop unique service propositions, creative service packages, and value-added solutions that differentiate the agency's digital content offerings, creative capabilities, and client deliverables in the competitive digital media landscape.
3. Client Acquisition: Implement client acquisition strategies, lead generation campaigns, and digital marketing tactics to attract new clients, nurture client relationships, and secure long-term partnerships with brands, businesses, and organizations seeking innovative digital content solutions.
4. Performance Measurement: Monitor campaign performance metrics, content engagement analytics, and client satisfaction scores to assess campaign effectiveness, content impact, and return on investment (ROI) for digital content creation services, marketing campaigns, and brand storytelling initiatives.

Further Resources:
- Digital Content Creation Strategies and Creative Production Techniques
- Visual Storytelling Best Practices and Multimedia Content Marketing Trends

66. Online Art Classes

Description: Launch an online platform offering art classes, creative workshops, and digital art tutorials for aspiring artists, hobbyists, and art enthusiasts seeking to enhance their artistic skills, explore new mediums, and cultivate creative talents in a virtual learning environment.

Marketing Insights and Opportunities:
- Art Education: Provide comprehensive art instruction, personalized mentoring, and skill-building exercises that cater to diverse artistic interests, skill levels, and learning objectives through online art courses, virtual workshops, and interactive learning experiences.
- Digital Accessibility: Expand access to art education, creative learning resources, and visual arts curriculum to global audiences, remote learners, and online communities interested in virtual art classes, digital art techniques, and multimedia art projects.
- Community Engagement: Foster a supportive learning community, artistic collaboration, and creative exchange among online students, art instructors, and creative professionals through peer feedback, virtual exhibitions, and collaborative art projects.

Requirements to Start:
- Artistic Expertise: Recruit qualified art instructors, professional artists, and industry experts proficient in various art mediums, digital art techniques, and creative teaching methods to facilitate engaging online art classes, live demonstrations, and interactive studio sessions.
- Technology Integration: Invest in digital learning platforms, video conferencing tools, and virtual classroom software that support online art instruction, multimedia presentations, and interactive teaching environments for real-time student engagement and virtual art education experiences.
- Curriculum Development: Design comprehensive art curricula, lesson plans, and instructional materials that align with artistic learning objectives, creative skill development, and educational standards in visual arts, drawing techniques, painting styles, and digital art mediums.

Challenges:
- Technical Support: Provide technical assistance, troubleshooting support, and online learning resources for students, educators, and virtual learners navigating digital art platforms, multimedia software, and virtual classroom technologies to ensure optimal learning experiences and student success in online art classes.
- Student Engagement: Enhance student participation, learning retention, and artistic motivation through interactive art activities, creative assignments, and collaborative projects that encourage artistic exploration, skill enhancement, and personal expression in virtual art education settings.
- Educational Accessibility: Address accessibility challenges, digital divide issues, and technological barriers to online art education by offering flexible learning options, mobile-friendly resources, and adaptive learning tools that accommodate diverse learning styles, educational needs, and artistic interests in virtual art classes.

Scalability Opportunities:
- Course Expansion: Expand art course offerings, specialization tracks, and continuing education programs to include advanced art techniques, specialized art mediums, and

interdisciplinary art subjects that attract diverse student demographics, lifelong learners, and professional artists seeking career development opportunities in the visual arts.
- Global Outreach: Promote online art classes, international art workshops, and virtual art exhibitions to global audiences, art communities, and cultural institutions interested in art education, creative learning experiences, and artistic skill development through digital art platforms, online learning environments, and virtual studio sessions.
- Collaborative Partnerships: Form strategic alliances with art schools, cultural organizations, and educational platforms to collaborate on joint initiatives, art education programs, and virtual learning projects that expand access to art resources, promote artistic innovation, and foster creative excellence in online art education.

Roadmap:
1. Curriculum Planning: Develop art curricula, instructional guides, and educational resources that support diverse art mediums, creative techniques, and artistic disciplines in online art classes, virtual workshops, and digital art courses.
2. Technology Integration: Implement digital learning tools, interactive teaching resources, and multimedia platforms for virtual art instruction, live demonstrations, and interactive studio sessions that enhance student engagement, artistic skill development, and creative learning outcomes in online art education.
3. Community Building: Cultivate a supportive learning community, artistic collaboration, and creative exchange among online students, art instructors, and professional artists through peer feedback, virtual critiques, and collaborative art projects that promote artistic growth, creative expression, and artistic development in virtual art classes.
4. Performance Evaluation: Monitor student progress, learning outcomes, and artistic achievements through assessment tools, portfolio reviews, and artistic evaluations to measure student proficiency, creative development, and educational success in online art education.

Further Resources:
- Online Art Education Strategies and Digital Learning Platforms
- Virtual Art Classes and Creative Skill Development Techniques

67. Podcast Production Studio

Description: Establish a podcast production studio offering podcast recording services, audio editing, content distribution, and podcast marketing solutions for podcasters, content creators, and businesses seeking to produce high-quality audio content and engage with their target audiences through podcasting platforms.

Marketing Insights and Opportunities:
- Podcast Industry: Tap into the growing popularity of podcasting, digital audio consumption trends, and podcast advertising opportunities by providing podcast production services, podcast hosting platforms, and audio content marketing strategies that enhance podcast visibility, listener engagement, and audience growth.

- Content Creation: Offer podcast recording sessions, audio editing services, and podcast production packages that cater to podcast creators, media professionals, and corporate clients interested in launching podcasts, producing episodic content, and distributing audio broadcasts on digital platforms.
- Audience Engagement: Leverage podcast analytics, listener feedback, and audience insights to optimize podcast content, improve listener retention, and increase podcast downloads through targeted content promotion, podcast marketing campaigns, and audience engagement strategies.

Requirements to Start:
- Studio Setup: Equip podcast production studios with professional recording equipment, audio mixing consoles, soundproofing materials, and podcast recording software that support podcast production workflows, audio editing processes, and content distribution strategies for podcast creators, media producers, and digital content creators.
- Technical Expertise: Hire skilled audio engineers, podcast producers, and multimedia specialists proficient in podcast editing, sound design, and audio mastering techniques to deliver high-quality podcast recordings, episode editing services, and audio production solutions that meet client specifications and industry standards.
- Creative Services: Provide creative services such as podcast scriptwriting, episode planning, guest coordination, and content scheduling to streamline podcast production workflows, optimize content creation processes, and ensure consistent podcast delivery across digital platforms and podcast directories.

Challenges:
- Competitive Landscape: Navigate the competitive podcast production market, emerging podcasting platforms, and evolving industry trends by offering differentiated podcast services, innovative content strategies, and customized podcast solutions that align with client objectives, audience preferences, and industry standards.
- Content Quality: Ensure audio clarity, podcast production excellence, and storytelling authenticity in podcast episodes, interview segments, and narrative-driven content that captivates listeners, enhances brand credibility, and fosters audience loyalty through engaging podcast experiences.
- Monetization Strategies: Develop monetization strategies, sponsorship opportunities, and revenue streams for podcast creators, brand advertisers, and corporate clients interested in podcast advertising, branded content partnerships, and monetization models that maximize podcast revenue potential and podcast ROI.

Scalability Opportunities:
- Service Expansion: Expand podcast production services, content distribution networks, and podcast marketing initiatives to new markets, international audiences, and industry sectors interested in podcast content creation, audio storytelling, and digital media production strategies.
- Podcast Network: Establish a podcast network, collaborative podcasting platforms, and cross-promotional opportunities with podcast creators, media partners, and industry influencers to amplify podcast reach, audience engagement, and brand visibility through podcast collaborations, content syndication, and strategic podcast partnerships.
- Technological Innovation: Embrace podcasting technology advancements, interactive podcast features, and podcasting tools that enhance podcast production

workflows, audience engagement experiences, and podcasting platforms' functionality for podcast creators, digital content producers, and media professionals.

Roadmap:
1. Market Research: Conduct market analysis, audience segmentation, and competitor analysis to identify podcasting trends, audience preferences, and industry insights driving demand for podcast production services, podcast marketing solutions, and audio content strategies.
2. Content Development: Develop podcast formats, episode structures, and thematic content themes that resonate with target audiences, align with client objectives, and showcase podcasting expertise, storytelling prowess, and creative storytelling strategies.
3. Client Acquisition: Implement client acquisition strategies, lead generation campaigns, and podcast marketing tactics to attract new clients, secure podcast production contracts, and build long-term partnerships with podcast creators, brand advertisers, and media agencies interested in podcast content creation, audio storytelling, and digital media production services.
4. Performance Evaluation: Measure podcast performance metrics, audience engagement analytics, and podcasting ROI to assess content effectiveness, optimize podcast strategies, and improve podcast distribution efforts for client campaigns, branded podcast initiatives, and podcast marketing campaigns.

Further Resources:
- Podcast Production Techniques and Audio Editing Tools
- Podcast Marketing Strategies and Audience Engagement Tactics

68. Video Production Services

Description: Establish a video production company providing comprehensive video production services including scriptwriting, filming, editing, and post-production services for corporate videos, promotional campaigns, and digital content creation projects.

Marketing Insights and Opportunities:
- Video Marketing: Capitalize on the growing demand for video content, video advertising, and digital storytelling by offering tailored video production services, branded video campaigns, and visual content strategies that enhance brand visibility, customer engagement, and audience reach.
- Content Diversity: Provide diverse video production solutions, video formats, and video styles that cater to corporate clients, small businesses, and digital marketers seeking professional video production services, creative storytelling techniques, and multimedia content strategies.
- Digital Engagement: Utilize video analytics, viewer engagement metrics, and video distribution channels to optimize video content performance, improve video campaign effectiveness, and maximize ROI through targeted video advertising, video SEO strategies, and video content marketing tactics.

Requirements to Start:

- Production Equipment: Invest in high-quality cameras, lighting equipment, audio recording tools, and video editing software that support professional video production workflows, cinematic storytelling techniques, and creative content creation processes for video projects, film productions, and digital media campaigns.
- Creative Talent: Recruit skilled videographers, video editors, scriptwriters, and production crew members proficient in video production techniques, visual storytelling skills, and multimedia content creation strategies to deliver impactful video content, promotional videos, and branded video campaigns that resonate with target audiences and achieve client objectives.
- Client Portfolio: Build a diverse client portfolio, industry partnerships, and referral networks through networking events, industry conferences, and client testimonials showcasing successful video production projects, corporate video campaigns, and digital content collaborations.

Challenges:
- Production Logistics: Manage production logistics, filming schedules, and video project timelines for multiple client projects, video shoots, and post-production processes that require effective project management, resource allocation, and client communication skills to ensure video quality, production efficiency, and client satisfaction.
- Creative Direction: Align creative vision, brand messaging, and storytelling concepts in video productions, promotional videos, and brand campaigns that capture audience attention, convey brand identity, and evoke emotional responses through compelling visual storytelling, narrative-driven content, and cinematic techniques.
- Budget Constraints: Navigate budget constraints, cost considerations, and financial planning challenges associated with video production costs, equipment rentals, and production expenses to deliver cost-effective video solutions, competitive pricing strategies, and value-added services that meet client budgets and project expectations.

Scalability Opportunities:
- Service Expansion: Expand video production services, video content offerings, and multimedia production capabilities to new markets, industry sectors, and global audiences interested in professional video services, digital storytelling strategies, and visual content marketing solutions that enhance brand visibility, customer engagement, and audience interaction.
- Technological Innovation: Embrace video technology advancements, video editing software updates, and video production trends that enhance video production workflows, streamline production processes, and optimize video content delivery for digital platforms, streaming services, and online distribution channels.
- Creative Collaboration: Collaborate with creative agencies, digital marketing firms, and media production studios to co-create video campaigns, branded video content, and integrated marketing strategies that leverage combined expertise, industry insights, and creative resources to achieve mutual business goals, client objectives, and campaign success.

Roadmap:
1. Market Analysis: Conduct market research, industry analysis, and client needs assessments to identify video production trends, audience preferences, and market opportunities driving demand for video production services, branded video campaigns, and digital content strategies.

2. Service Differentiation: Develop unique service propositions, creative video packages, and value-added solutions that differentiate the video production company's offerings, showcase creative capabilities, and deliver compelling video content that resonates with target audiences, aligns with brand messaging, and achieves client objectives.
3. Client Acquisition: Implement client acquisition strategies, lead generation campaigns, and digital marketing tactics to attract new clients, secure video production contracts, and foster long-term partnerships with corporate clients, marketing agencies, and digital brands interested in video content creation, promotional video campaigns, and multimedia production services.
4. Performance Measurement: Monitor video performance metrics, audience engagement analytics, and video campaign effectiveness to evaluate video content impact, optimize video strategies, and measure ROI for video production projects, branded video campaigns, and digital media initiatives.

Further Resources:
- Video Production Techniques and Creative Filmmaking Strategies
- Branded Video Content Strategies and Video Marketing Campaigns

69. Graphic Design and Branding Agency

Description: Establish a graphic design and branding agency offering creative services including logo design, brand identity development, marketing collateral design, and visual branding solutions for businesses, startups, and organizations seeking to enhance brand recognition, market presence, and customer engagement through effective visual communication strategies.

Marketing Insights and Opportunities:
- Brand Positioning: Help clients define brand positioning, brand differentiation, and market positioning through strategic brand identity design, visual storytelling techniques, and brand messaging strategies that resonate with target audiences, communicate brand values, and establish brand authority in competitive markets.
- Visual Communication: Offer graphic design services, creative branding solutions, and visual content strategies that integrate typography, color theory, and graphic elements to create cohesive brand identities, marketing materials, and digital assets that reinforce brand consistency, enhance brand recognition, and drive brand loyalty.
- Market Demand: Address the growing demand for graphic design services, branding consultancy, and visual communication solutions among businesses, startups, and corporate clients looking to revamp brand aesthetics, refresh marketing materials, and optimize brand performance through innovative design concepts, creative branding strategies, and visual storytelling initiatives.

Requirements to Start:
- Creative Expertise: Recruit skilled graphic designers, brand strategists, creative directors, and visual artists proficient in graphic design principles, brand identity development, and visual communication techniques to deliver impactful brand designs, marketing collateral, and visual branding solutions that align with client objectives, brand goals, and market expectations.

- Design Tools: Invest in graphic design software, digital illustration tools, typography resources, and design resources that support creative design workflows, visual branding projects, and brand identity development processes for clients across diverse industries, market segments, and business sectors.
- Client Collaboration: Foster collaborative client relationships, client engagement opportunities, and client feedback loops through design consultations, brand workshops, and brand discovery sessions that facilitate client input, creative direction, and brand vision alignment in graphic design projects, brand identity designs, and visual branding initiatives.

Challenges:
- Creative Briefs: Interpret client briefs, design requirements, and brand guidelines to develop custom design concepts, brand aesthetics, and visual identity systems that capture brand essence, communicate brand narratives, and resonate with target audiences through compelling graphic designs, memorable logos, and impactful brand visuals.
- Project Timelines: Manage project timelines, design deliverables, and client expectations for multiple design projects, branding campaigns, and creative assignments that require efficient project management, creative workflow optimization, and client communication strategies to ensure design quality, brand consistency, and project success.
- Market Differentiation: Differentiate agency offerings, creative design services, and visual branding solutions from competitors through innovative design concepts, strategic brand positioning, and brand storytelling techniques that showcase design expertise, creative capabilities, and brand identity craftsmanship in graphic design projects, branding campaigns, and visual communication strategies.

Scalability Opportunities:
- Service Expansion: Expand graphic design services, branding consultancy offerings, and visual communication solutions to new markets, industry verticals, and global audiences interested in creative design services, brand identity development, and visual branding strategies that enhance brand visibility, market competitiveness, and customer engagement through innovative design concepts, brand storytelling initiatives, and creative brand experiences.
- Brand Partnerships: Form strategic alliances with marketing agencies, advertising firms, and digital media partners to collaborate on integrated marketing campaigns, brand activation strategies, and cross-channel branding initiatives that leverage combined expertise, industry insights, and creative resources to drive brand growth, market expansion, and business success.
- Creative Innovation: Embrace design technology advancements, graphic design trends, and visual communication innovations that enhance design capabilities, streamline design workflows, and optimize design processes for graphic design projects, branding campaigns, and visual storytelling initiatives in digital media, print media, and online platforms.

Roadmap:
1. Market Research: Conduct market analysis, brand audits, and competitor research to identify industry trends, client needs, and market opportunities driving demand for graphic design services, branding consultancy, and visual communication strategies.

2. Creative Strategy: Develop creative briefs, design proposals, and brand identity concepts that articulate client objectives, brand visions, and design aesthetics through strategic brand positioning, visual storytelling techniques, and brand identity systems that resonate with target audiences, communicate brand values, and elevate brand equity.
3. Client Acquisition: Implement client acquisition strategies, lead generation campaigns, and digital marketing tactics to attract new clients, secure design contracts, and build long-term partnerships with businesses, startups, and organizations seeking graphic design services, branding solutions, and visual communication strategies to enhance brand recognition, market differentiation, and customer engagement.
4. Performance Evaluation: Measure design performance metrics, brand engagement analytics, and client satisfaction scores to evaluate design effectiveness, optimize design strategies, and improve design outcomes for graphic design projects, branding campaigns, and visual communication initiatives.

Further Resources:
- Graphic Design Principles and Creative Branding Techniques
- Visual Communication Strategies and Brand Identity Development

70. Photography Studio

Description: Establish a photography studio offering professional photography services including portrait photography, event photography, product photography, and commercial photography for individuals, businesses, and organizations looking to capture memorable moments, showcase products, and enhance brand imagery through high-quality photographic storytelling and visual content creation.

Marketing Insights and Opportunities:
- Visual Storytelling: Harness the power of visual storytelling, creative composition, and photographic techniques to convey compelling narratives, evoke emotional responses, and showcase authentic moments that resonate with target audiences, communicate brand stories, and elevate brand identity through professional photography services, visual content strategies, and creative image campaigns.
- Market Demand: Address the growing demand for professional photography services, commercial photography solutions, and digital content creation among businesses, marketing agencies, and corporate clients seeking impactful visuals, engaging photography, and visual storytelling techniques that capture attention, inspire action, and drive brand engagement through visual media, online platforms, and digital marketing channels.
- Photographic Excellence: Provide diverse photography services, specialized photography packages, and custom photography solutions that cater to client preferences, industry specifications, and creative briefs for capturing professional portraits, corporate events, product launches, and brand campaigns with a focus on aesthetic appeal, visual clarity, and creative vision in photographic storytelling, image composition, and visual content creation.

Requirements to Start:

- Photography Equipment: Invest in professional cameras, lenses, lighting equipment, and photography accessories that support versatile photography styles, technical proficiency, and creative photography techniques for capturing professional portraits, commercial images, and creative visual content that meets client expectations, industry standards, and aesthetic requirements.

- Studio Space: Secure a dedicated photography studio space, creative workspace, or on-location shooting environments equipped with essential photography tools, studio props, and technical resources to facilitate photography sessions, client consultations, and creative brainstorming sessions for planning, executing, and delivering professional photography services, visual content projects, and brand photography campaigns.

- Creative Team: Recruit skilled photographers, photo editors, and photography assistants with expertise in portrait photography, event coverage, product imaging, and commercial photography techniques to collaborate on photography projects, manage photo shoots, and deliver exceptional photographic results, visual storytelling experiences, and creative imagery that capture moments, convey emotions, and amplify brand presence through professional photography services, visual content strategies, and image-based storytelling initiatives.

Challenges:
- Client Expectations: Manage client expectations, photography briefs, and project specifications for diverse photography assignments, creative campaigns, and visual content projects requiring effective communication, creative direction, and client collaboration to achieve photographic excellence, client satisfaction, and brand success through professional photography services, creative imaging solutions, and visual storytelling strategies.

- Technical Expertise: Enhance technical proficiency, photography skills, and image editing capabilities through continuous learning, professional development, and creative training programs that empower photographers, creative teams, and photography professionals to master photography techniques, refine visual styles, and elevate photographic storytelling through innovative approaches, artistic perspectives, and creative insights in visual content creation, commercial photography, and brand imaging initiatives.

- Market Competition: Navigate competitive photography markets, digital photography trends, and industry advancements by offering distinctive photography services, specialized photography packages, and custom visual content solutions that differentiate the photography studio, showcase artistic craftsmanship, and deliver memorable photographic experiences, brand imagery, and visual storytelling campaigns that captivate audiences, inspire action, and drive brand engagement through professional photography services, commercial photography solutions, and visual content creation strategies.

Scalability Opportunities:
- Service Expansion: Expand photography services, creative photography offerings, and visual content solutions to new markets, industry sectors, and global audiences interested in professional photography services, digital imaging solutions, and visual storytelling techniques that enhance brand visibility, market positioning, and customer engagement through strategic photography campaigns, creative imaging projects, and visual content initiatives that leverage photography expertise, creative vision, and technical proficiency in capturing moments, conveying emotions, and amplifying

brand presence through visual media, online platforms, and digital marketing channels.
- Client Relationships: Build lasting client relationships, industry partnerships, and collaborative alliances through photography workshops, networking events, and client engagement initiatives that foster trust, inspire creativity, and cultivate brand loyalty among businesses, marketing agencies, and corporate clients seeking professional photography services, commercial photography solutions, and visual content creation strategies that enhance brand identity, communicate brand stories, and elevate brand recognition through visual storytelling, photographic excellence, and creative image campaigns that capture attention, inspire action, and drive brand engagement through professional photography services, visual content strategies, and creative image campaigns.

Roadmap:
1. Market Analysis: Conduct market research, client surveys, and industry analysis to identify photography trends, client preferences, and market opportunities driving demand for professional photography services, commercial photography solutions, and visual content creation strategies.
2. Creative Strategy: Develop creative concepts, photography packages, and visual content ideas that align with client objectives, industry trends, and creative briefs for producing compelling photographic storytelling, capturing memorable moments, and delivering creative photography campaigns that resonate with target audiences, communicate brand narratives, and elevate brand identity through professional photography services, commercial photography solutions, and visual content creation strategies that capture attention, inspire action, and drive brand engagement through professional photography services, visual content strategies, and creative image campaigns.
3. Client Acquisition: Implement client acquisition strategies, lead generation campaigns, and digital marketing tactics to attract new clients, secure photography contracts, and build long-term partnerships with businesses, marketing agencies, and corporate clients interested in professional photography services, commercial photography solutions, and visual content creation strategies that enhance brand recognition, communicate brand stories, and elevate brand identity through professional photography services, visual content strategies, and creative image campaigns.
4. Performance Measurement: Monitor photography performance metrics, client feedback, and project outcomes to evaluate photography effectiveness, optimize photography strategies, and improve photography results for professional photography services, commercial photography solutions, and visual content creation strategies that enhance brand visibility, communicate brand stories, and elevate brand identity through professional photography services, visual content strategies, and creative image campaigns.

Further Resources:
- Professional Photography Techniques and Creative Imaging Strategies
- Visual Storytelling Principles and Brand Photography Best Practices

Real Estate and Property Businesses

Starting a business in real estate and property involves providing essential services that cater to property management, vacation rental management, sustainable architecture, and more. These ventures aim to meet the diverse needs of property owners, investors, and tenants while promoting sustainability and efficiency in building practices.

71. Property Management Services

Description: Launch a property management company offering comprehensive management services for residential, commercial, and industrial properties. Services may include property maintenance, tenant management, rent collection, and financial reporting.

Marketing Insights and Opportunities:
- Property Portfolio Management: Assist property owners in maximizing the value of their real estate investments through efficient property management, strategic tenant placement, and proactive maintenance services that enhance property profitability, tenant satisfaction, and long-term investment returns.
- Rental Market Trends: Capitalize on rental market trends, occupancy rates, and rental property demand by offering tailored property management solutions, rental property marketing strategies, and tenant retention programs that attract qualified tenants, minimize vacancy rates, and optimize rental property performance through proactive leasing, property maintenance, and tenant relations.

Requirements to Start:
- Property Management Software: Invest in property management software, accounting tools, and digital platforms that streamline property operations, automate rent collection processes, and facilitate tenant communication for effective property management, lease administration, and financial reporting.
- Maintenance Team: Hire qualified maintenance technicians, property inspectors, and repair contractors capable of performing routine property inspections, emergency repairs, and preventative maintenance services that ensure property safety, operational efficiency, and tenant satisfaction through responsive property management, reliable maintenance solutions, and proactive tenant support.
- Client Relationships: Build strong client relationships, tenant partnerships, and community connections through personalized property management services, tenant engagement initiatives, and landlord-tenant mediation efforts that foster trust, enhance communication, and resolve issues promptly in rental property management, commercial property management, and residential property operations.

Challenges:
- Regulatory Compliance: Navigate regulatory requirements, landlord-tenant laws, and property management regulations governing rental property operations, lease agreements, and eviction procedures to ensure legal compliance, tenant rights protection, and property owner liability management in property management services, rental property management, and commercial real estate management.

- Tenant Relations: Manage tenant disputes, lease negotiations, and tenant expectations in rental property management, commercial property management, and residential property operations that require effective communication, conflict resolution skills, and tenant satisfaction strategies to maintain positive tenant relations, minimize tenant turnover, and promote tenant retention through responsive property management, quality customer service, and tenant engagement initiatives.
- Financial Management: Monitor property finances, budget planning, and rental income projections for rental property management, commercial property management, and residential property operations that require financial transparency, expense tracking, and budget management skills to optimize property profitability, maximize rental property returns, and achieve financial success through effective property management, strategic asset management, and proactive investment strategies.

Scalability Opportunities:
- Service Expansion: Expand property management services, real estate management solutions, and asset management offerings to new markets, geographic regions, and property sectors interested in professional property management, commercial real estate services, and residential property management solutions that enhance property value, improve tenant satisfaction, and optimize rental property performance through comprehensive property management, proactive asset management, and strategic investment strategies.
- Technology Integration: Embrace property management technology, digital platforms, and real estate software solutions that enhance property operations, streamline property management processes, and optimize tenant management practices for rental property management, commercial property management, and residential property operations that require advanced property management tools, cloud-based solutions, and mobile applications to deliver efficient property services, tenant engagement solutions, and property performance metrics through proactive property management, quality customer service, and tenant relationship management.

Roadmap:
1. Market Analysis: Conduct market research, property analysis, and competitive benchmarking to identify property management trends, rental market dynamics, and investment opportunities driving demand for property management services, commercial real estate management, and residential property operations.
2. Service Differentiation: Develop unique service propositions, property management packages, and value-added solutions that differentiate the property management company, showcase industry expertise, and deliver comprehensive property management services, rental property solutions, and asset management strategies that optimize property performance, maximize rental property returns, and achieve client objectives through proactive property management, tenant retention programs, and quality customer service.
3. Client Acquisition: Implement client acquisition strategies, lead generation campaigns, and digital marketing tactics to attract new clients, secure property management contracts, and build long-term partnerships with property owners, real estate investors, and institutional clients interested in property management services, commercial property management solutions, and residential property management strategies that enhance property value, improve tenant satisfaction, and optimize rental

property operations through proactive property management, asset management services, and investment management strategies.

4. Performance Measurement: Monitor property performance metrics, rental property analytics, and tenant satisfaction surveys to evaluate property management effectiveness, optimize property management strategies, and improve property outcomes for property management services, rental property management solutions, and commercial real estate operations that achieve property profitability, tenant retention goals, and client satisfaction through proactive property management, strategic asset management, and investment management solutions.

Further Resources:
- Property Management Best Practices and Rental Property Management Strategies
- Commercial Real Estate Management and Residential Property Operations

72. Vacation Rental Management

Description: Establish a vacation rental management company offering full-service management solutions for vacation homes, rental properties, and short-term rentals. Services may include property listing management, guest communication, cleaning services, and booking management.

Marketing Insights and Opportunities:
- Vacation Rental Market: Tap into the growing vacation rental market, traveler preferences, and seasonal booking trends by offering personalized vacation rental management services, property marketing strategies, and guest experience enhancements that attract travelers, maximize occupancy rates, and optimize rental property performance through professional vacation rental management, property management solutions, and guest services.
- Property Marketing: Utilize digital marketing channels, online booking platforms, and vacation rental websites to promote vacation rental properties, showcase property amenities, and highlight unique selling points that appeal to vacationers, attract bookings, and generate rental income through effective vacation rental marketing, property listing optimization, and guest booking management strategies.

Requirements to Start:
- Vacation Rental Software: Invest in vacation rental software, booking management tools, and property management platforms that streamline vacation rental operations, automate guest communications, and simplify booking processes for vacation rental management, property listing management, and guest experience enhancements that enhance property visibility, increase booking inquiries, and optimize rental property performance through professional vacation rental management, property management solutions, and guest services.
- Property Maintenance: Coordinate property maintenance, housekeeping services, and guest accommodations for vacation rental properties, short-term rentals, and holiday homes that require routine property inspections, cleaning services, and maintenance checks to ensure property readiness, guest satisfaction, and operational efficiency through proactive vacation rental management, property management solutions, and guest services.

- Guest Relations: Provide personalized guest experiences, hospitality services, and concierge amenities for vacation rental guests, travelers, and holidaymakers seeking memorable vacation experiences, luxury accommodations, and exclusive property amenities that exceed guest expectations, improve guest satisfaction, and enhance vacation rental profitability through professional vacation rental management, property management solutions, and guest services.

Challenges:
- Seasonal Demand: Manage seasonal demand, peak booking periods, and vacation rental occupancy rates for vacation rental properties, short-term rentals, and holiday homes that require effective pricing strategies, booking management solutions, and marketing campaigns to attract travelers, maximize rental income, and optimize property performance through professional vacation rental management, property management solutions, and guest services.
- Property Regulations: Navigate vacation rental regulations, zoning laws, and local ordinances governing vacation rental operations, property management practices, and short-term rental policies to ensure compliance, regulatory compliance, and legal liability management in vacation rental management, property management solutions, and guest services.
- Guest Expectations: Address guest inquiries, booking requests, and vacation rental accommodations for vacation rental guests, travelers, and holidaymakers seeking comfortable stays, exceptional service, and memorable experiences through responsive guest communications, hospitality services, and concierge amenities that enhance guest satisfaction, improve guest loyalty, and optimize vacation rental profitability through professional vacation rental management, property management solutions, and guest services.

Scalability Opportunities:
- Service Expansion: Expand vacation rental services, property management solutions, and guest experience enhancements to new markets, travel destinations, and global audiences interested in vacation rental properties, short-term rentals, and holiday homes that offer unique accommodations, luxury amenities, and personalized guest experiences through professional vacation rental management, property management solutions, and guest services.
- Technology Integration: Embrace vacation rental technology, property management software, and booking platforms that streamline vacation rental operations, automate booking processes, and enhance guest experiences for vacation rental guests, travelers, and holidaymakers seeking seamless stays, convenient accommodations, and memorable vacation experiences through professional vacation rental management, property management solutions, and guest services.

Roadmap:
1. Market Analysis: Conduct market research, vacation rental analysis, and guest behavior studies to identify vacation rental trends, traveler preferences, and booking trends driving demand for vacation rental management services, property management solutions, and guest experience enhancements through professional vacation rental management, property management solutions, and guest services.
2. Service Differentiation: Develop unique service propositions, vacation rental packages, and guest experience enhancements that differentiate the vacation rental management company, showcase property expertise, and deliver personalized guest

experiences, luxury accommodations, and exclusive property amenities through professional vacation rental management, property management solutions, and guest services.
3. Client Acquisition: Implement client acquisition strategies, digital marketing campaigns, and online booking tactics to attract new property owners, secure vacation rental contracts, and build long-term partnerships with travelers, vacationers, and holidaymakers seeking vacation rental properties, short-term rentals, and holiday homes that offer memorable vacation experiences, exceptional service, and exclusive amenities through professional vacation rental management, property management solutions, and guest services.

73. Sustainable Architecture Firm

Description: Launch a sustainable architecture firm specializing in eco-friendly building design, green construction practices, and environmentally responsible architectural solutions. Services may include sustainable design consultations, green building certifications, and renewable energy integration.

Marketing Insights and Opportunities:
- Environmental Sustainability: Capitalize on the growing demand for sustainable building practices, green architecture solutions, and eco-friendly design principles that prioritize environmental conservation, energy efficiency, and carbon footprint reduction through sustainable architecture projects, green building certifications, and renewable energy initiatives.
- Client Preferences: Address client preferences, industry trends, and regulatory requirements driving demand for sustainable architecture firms, green building designs, and environmentally responsible architectural solutions that enhance building performance, promote resource conservation, and support sustainable development goals through innovative architecture designs, green building certifications, and renewable energy technologies.

Requirements to Start:
- Green Design Expertise: Develop expertise in sustainable architecture, green building principles, and eco-friendly design strategies that integrate renewable materials, energy-efficient technologies, and passive solar design techniques for optimizing building performance, reducing environmental impact, and achieving green building certifications through sustainable architecture projects, environmental consulting services, and green building initiatives.
- Collaborative Partnerships: Form strategic partnerships with green builders, renewable energy providers, and environmental consultants to support sustainable architecture projects, green building certifications, and eco-friendly design solutions that enhance building efficiency, improve indoor air quality, and promote environmental stewardship through sustainable architecture projects, green building certifications, and eco-friendly design initiatives.
- Client Relationships: Build client relationships, industry connections, and community engagements through sustainable architecture workshops, green building seminars, and environmental outreach programs that educate clients, promote sustainable living practices, and advocate for green building designs through

sustainable architecture projects, green building certifications, and eco-friendly design initiatives.

Challenges:
- Regulatory Compliance: Navigate green building regulations, environmental standards, and sustainable design guidelines governing sustainable architecture practices, green building certifications, and eco-friendly construction techniques to ensure compliance, regulatory approval, and environmental stewardship in sustainable architecture projects, green building certifications, and environmental consulting services.
- Technology Integration: Embrace sustainable architecture technology, green building software, and environmental monitoring tools that enhance building performance, optimize energy efficiency, and support eco-friendly design practices through sustainable architecture projects, green building certifications, and renewable energy initiatives.

Scalability Opportunities:
- Market Expansion: Expand sustainable architecture services, green building designs, and eco-friendly design solutions to new markets, geographic regions, and global audiences interested in sustainable architecture firms, green building certifications, and environmental consulting services that promote sustainability, improve building efficiency, and support green building initiatives through sustainable architecture projects, green building certifications, and eco-friendly design solutions.
- Innovation Leadership: Lead industry innovation, sustainable design trends, and green building technologies by offering cutting-edge sustainable architecture solutions, green building designs, and eco-friendly design strategies that advance building performance, optimize energy efficiency, and promote environmental stewardship through sustainable architecture projects, green building certifications, and renewable energy initiatives.

Roadmap:
1. Market Analysis: Conduct market research, sustainable architecture analysis, and green building surveys to identify market trends, client preferences, and regulatory requirements driving demand for sustainable architecture firms, green building certifications, and eco-friendly design solutions through sustainable architecture projects, green building certifications, and environmental consulting services.
2. Service Differentiation: Develop unique service propositions, sustainable architecture designs, and eco-friendly design strategies that differentiate the sustainable architecture firm, showcase industry expertise, and deliver sustainable architecture projects, green building certifications, and environmental consulting services through sustainable architecture projects, green building certifications, and eco-friendly design solutions.
3. Client Acquisition: Implement client acquisition strategies, environmental marketing campaigns, and sustainable architecture promotions to attract new clients, secure sustainable architecture contracts, and build long-term partnerships with property owners, real estate developers, and institutional clients interested in sustainable architecture firms, green building certifications, and environmental consulting services through sustainable architecture projects, green building certifications, and eco-friendly design solutions.

4. Performance Measurement: Monitor sustainable architecture metrics, green building performance, and environmental impact assessments to evaluate sustainable architecture effectiveness, optimize green building strategies, and improve sustainable architecture outcomes for sustainable architecture firms, green building certifications, and eco-friendly design solutions through sustainable architecture projects, green building certifications, and environmental consulting services.

Further Resources:
- Sustainable Architecture Principles and Green Building Design Strategies
- Environmental Stewardship and Green Building Practices

74. Real Estate Investment Trust (REIT)

Description: Establish a Real Estate Investment Trust (REIT) that allows investors to pool funds to invest in income-generating real estate properties such as commercial buildings, apartments, or retail spaces. REITs typically pay out dividends to investors from the rental income earned from these properties.

Marketing Insights and Opportunities:
- Investment Diversification: Attract investors seeking diversification through real estate investments without direct property ownership responsibilities. Highlight the stable income potential, portfolio diversification benefits, and tax advantages of investing in REITs over direct property ownership.
- Sector Specific REITs: Focus on specialized REITs such as healthcare facilities, industrial warehouses, or residential rentals to target specific investor preferences and capitalize on sector-specific market opportunities.

Requirements to Start:
- Legal Structure: Establish a legal structure compliant with REIT regulations, which typically require distributing at least 90% of taxable income as dividends to shareholders.
- Property Portfolio: Acquire a portfolio of income-producing properties that meet REIT eligibility criteria, such as minimum asset and income requirements.
- Investor Relations: Develop strong investor relations strategies to attract and retain shareholders through transparent communication, regular dividends, and potential for capital appreciation.

Challenges:
- Market Volatility: Navigate market fluctuations and economic cycles that may impact property values and rental income, affecting dividend payouts to investors.
- Regulatory Compliance: Adhere to complex regulatory requirements governing REIT operations, including asset diversification, income distribution, and tax treatment.

Scalability Opportunities:
- Portfolio Expansion: Expand the property portfolio by acquiring additional income-generating properties to increase dividend payouts and attract new investors.

- Geographic Diversification: Diversify geographically to mitigate risks associated with regional economic downturns or local market fluctuations.

Roadmap:
1. Market Analysis: Conduct thorough market research to identify target investors, assess market demand for specific property types, and evaluate potential acquisition opportunities.
2. Legal Compliance: Establish a REIT structure compliant with regulatory requirements, including IRS regulations for tax-exempt status and SEC guidelines for public offerings.
3. Property Acquisition: Acquire income-producing properties that align with REIT investment objectives and asset diversification strategies.
4. Investor Engagement: Implement investor relations programs to attract and retain shareholders, including regular financial reporting, dividend distributions, and transparency in investment decisions.

75. Home Staging Services

Description: Start a home staging business that prepares residential properties for sale by enhancing their appeal to potential buyers. Services may include furniture rental, interior design consultation, and space optimization.

Marketing Insights and Opportunities:
- Real Estate Agent Partnerships: Partner with real estate agents to offer home staging as a value-added service to their clients, potentially increasing property sales prices and reducing time on market.
- Virtual Staging: Expand services to include virtual staging for online listings, catering to the growing trend of digital house hunting.

Requirements to Start:
- Inventory: Acquire a collection of furniture, decor items, and accessories for staging various types of homes.
- Design Expertise: Employ skilled interior designers or decorators capable of transforming spaces to appeal to target demographics and buyer preferences.

Challenges:
- Client Expectations: Meet client expectations while working within budget constraints and tight timelines.
- Logistics: Manage logistics involved in furniture delivery, setup, and removal after the sale.

Scalability Opportunities:
- Market Expansion: Expand into neighboring markets or offer virtual staging services to reach a broader audience.
- Partnerships: Forge partnerships with real estate developers or property management companies for staging model homes or rental properties.

Roadmap:

1. Market Research: Identify local market demand for home staging services and competitive landscape.
2. Service Offerings: Develop pricing packages and service offerings tailored to different property types and client needs.
3. Marketing Strategy: Implement marketing strategies to reach real estate agents, property sellers, and online platforms where potential buyers search for properties.
4. Client Relationships: Build strong relationships with real estate professionals and leverage client testimonials to build credibility.

76. Property Inspection Services

Description: Launch a property inspection business offering thorough inspections of residential and commercial properties. Services may include pre-purchase inspections, rental property assessments, and building code compliance checks.

Marketing Insights and Opportunities:
- Real Estate Transactions: Position services as essential for buyers, sellers, and real estate agents to ensure property condition transparency and informed decision-making.
- Specialized Inspections: Offer niche services such as energy efficiency audits or mold inspections to cater to specific client needs.

Requirements to Start:
- Certification: Obtain certifications or licenses required by state or local regulations for property inspectors.
- Equipment: Invest in inspection tools and software for thorough assessments and detailed reporting.

Challenges:
- Liability: Mitigate risks associated with providing accurate property condition assessments and potential legal implications.
- Competitive Market: Differentiate services from competitors offering similar inspection services.

Scalability Opportunities:
- Expansion: Expand services to include additional inspection types or geographic areas.
- Technology Integration: Incorporate technology for streamlined scheduling, reporting, and client communication.

Roadmap:
1. Training and Certification: Complete required training and certifications to become a licensed property inspector.
2. Business Setup: Establish legal structure, insurance coverage, and operational procedures.
3. Marketing and Networking: Build relationships with real estate professionals and develop marketing materials to promote services.

4. Service Excellence: Focus on delivering high-quality inspections, detailed reports, and excellent customer service to build reputation and referrals.

Manufacturing and Production Businesses

Starting a business in manufacturing and production involves creating tangible products ranging from custom furniture to biodegradable products and offering specialized services like 3D printing.

77. 3D Printing Services

Description: Establish a 3D printing service that provides custom manufacturing solutions using additive manufacturing technology. Services may include prototyping, production of customized parts, and creative design solutions.

Marketing Insights and Opportunities:
- Customization: Highlight the ability to create bespoke products tailored to individual customer specifications, catering to industries such as healthcare, automotive, and consumer goods.
- Rapid Prototyping: Offer rapid prototyping services to startups and product developers seeking to iterate designs quickly and cost-effectively.

Requirements to Start:
- Equipment: Invest in high-quality 3D printers capable of producing detailed and functional prototypes or end-use parts.
- Technical Expertise: Employ skilled technicians or engineers proficient in CAD (Computer-Aided Design) software and additive manufacturing techniques.

Challenges:
- Material Selection: Navigate the complexities of material selection suitable for various applications, ensuring durability, flexibility, or biocompatibility as needed.
- Technological Advancements: Stay updated with advancements in 3D printing technology and software to remain competitive in the market.

Scalability Opportunities:
- Industry Partnerships: Forge partnerships with designers, engineers, and businesses across different sectors to expand service offerings and client base.
- Vertical Integration: Consider vertical integration by offering related services such as post-processing, finishing, or assembly to add value and increase revenue.

Roadmap:
1. Market Research: Identify target industries and applications for 3D printing services, assess competition, and understand customer needs.
2. Equipment Acquisition: Purchase or lease 3D printing equipment suitable for initial operations and future scalability.
3. Service Development: Define service offerings, pricing models, and turnaround times based on market demand and technological capabilities.
4. Marketing Strategy: Develop a marketing plan to reach target customers through online platforms, industry events, and partnerships with local businesses.

78. Custom Furniture Design

Description: Start a business specializing in custom furniture design and manufacturing, offering unique pieces tailored to client preferences and interior spaces.

Marketing Insights and Opportunities:
- Personalization: Emphasize the ability to create one-of-a-kind furniture pieces that reflect individual style and functional needs.
- Interior Design Partnerships: Collaborate with interior designers to offer bespoke furniture solutions for residential and commercial projects.

Requirements to Start:
- Design Expertise: Employ skilled furniture designers capable of translating client visions into functional and aesthetically pleasing designs.
- Workshop Space: Secure a workshop equipped with woodworking tools, upholstery equipment, and finishing materials.

Challenges:
- Production Time: Manage production timelines and client expectations, balancing craftsmanship with efficiency.
- Material Sourcing: Establish relationships with reliable suppliers for high-quality materials such as hardwood, upholstery fabrics, and sustainable options.

Scalability Opportunities:
- E-commerce Expansion: Expand reach through an online platform showcasing portfolio, customization options, and client testimonials.
- Product Line Diversification: Introduce complementary products such as home accessories or bespoke cabinetry to broaden market appeal.

Roadmap:
1. Design Portfolio: Develop a portfolio showcasing past projects, design capabilities, and craftsmanship to attract prospective clients.
2. Client Relationships: Build strong client relationships through personalized consultations, design revisions, and transparent communication.
3. Marketing and Promotion: Utilize digital marketing strategies, social media platforms, and participation in trade shows or local events to promote custom furniture services.
4. Operational Efficiency: Implement efficient workflow processes, quality control measures, and inventory management systems to streamline production and meet client deadlines.

79. Biodegradable Product Manufacturing

Description: Launch a manufacturing business focused on producing biodegradable products, such as packaging materials, utensils, or personal care items that minimize environmental impact.

Marketing Insights and Opportunities:
- Environmental Consciousness: Appeal to eco-conscious consumers and businesses seeking sustainable alternatives to traditional plastic products.
- Regulatory Compliance: Ensure products meet environmental standards and certifications for biodegradability and compostability.

Requirements to Start:
- Research and Development: Invest in R&D for biodegradable materials, formulations, and production processes.
- Production Facility: Establish a manufacturing facility equipped for bioplastic extrusion, molding, or other manufacturing techniques.

Challenges:
- Material Performance: Balance biodegradability with product functionality, durability, and cost-effectiveness.
- Supply Chain Sustainability: Source raw materials from sustainable suppliers and manage logistics to minimize environmental footprint.

Scalability Opportunities:
- Product Innovation: Continuously innovate with new biodegradable product offerings and improvements in material performance.
- Partnerships and Distribution: Collaborate with retailers, distributors, and eco-friendly brands to expand market reach and distribution channels.

Roadmap:
1. Market Analysis: Identify target markets, consumer preferences, and competitive landscape for biodegradable products.
2. Material Development: Develop or collaborate with suppliers on bioplastic formulations and material sourcing strategies.
3. Manufacturing Setup: Configure production lines, implement quality control measures, and ensure compliance with environmental regulations.
4. Marketing Strategy: Launch campaigns highlighting product benefits, sustainability credentials, and environmental impact to attract environmentally conscious consumers and businesses.

80. Organic Skincare Product Line

Description: Launch a business focused on producing organic skincare products, including cleansers, moisturizers, serums, and more, catering to consumers' increasing demand for natural and eco-friendly beauty solutions.

Marketing Insights and Opportunities:
- Growing Demand: Tap into the rising consumer preference for organic, cruelty-free, and environmentally sustainable skincare options.

- E-commerce Presence: Utilize online platforms and social media channels to reach a broader audience and educate consumers about the benefits of organic skincare.

Requirements to Start:
- Formulation Expertise: Develop or collaborate with skincare chemists to create effective formulations using organic ingredients.
- Certifications: Obtain necessary certifications for organic skincare products to enhance credibility and appeal to health-conscious consumers.

Challenges:
- Ingredient Sourcing: Establish reliable supply chains for organic ingredients while ensuring sustainability and quality.
- Regulatory Compliance: Navigate regulations related to skincare product formulation, labeling, and marketing claims.

Scalability Opportunities:
- Product Expansion: Introduce new skincare products such as masks, sunscreens, or specialty treatments to diversify product offerings.
- Retail Partnerships: Partner with natural health stores, spas, and beauty retailers to expand distribution channels and reach new customer segments.

Roadmap:
1. Market Research: Conduct market research to identify target demographics, competitor analysis, and market trends in organic skincare.
2. Product Development: Develop skincare formulations, packaging designs, and branding strategies aligned with consumer preferences and market demands.
3. Production Setup: Establish manufacturing processes, quality control measures, and packaging solutions that uphold organic standards and product integrity.
4. Marketing and Sales: Launch marketing campaigns emphasizing product benefits, eco-friendly practices, and organic certifications to build brand awareness and customer loyalty.

81. Specialty Chemical Manufacturing

Description: Start a specialty chemical manufacturing business that produces customized chemical solutions for industrial, commercial, or scientific applications, catering to specific client needs and industry requirements.

Marketing Insights and Opportunities:
- Niche Markets: Target industries requiring specialized chemical formulations such as pharmaceuticals, electronics, or agricultural chemicals.
- Customization: Highlight capabilities in customizing chemical compositions and formulations to meet client specifications and industry standards.

Requirements to Start:
- Chemical Expertise: Employ chemical engineers or specialists with expertise in formulation development, quality control, and regulatory compliance.

- Production Facility: Secure a manufacturing facility equipped with specialized equipment for chemical synthesis, blending, and packaging.

Challenges:
- Safety and Compliance: Adhere to stringent safety protocols, environmental regulations, and industry standards governing chemical manufacturing and handling.
- Technical Complexity: Address challenges related to chemical stability, shelf-life, and compatibility with diverse applications and materials.

Scalability Opportunities:
- Research and Development: Invest in R&D to innovate new chemical formulations, improve existing products, and address emerging market needs.
- Global Expansion: Explore international markets and partnerships to scale operations and reach a broader customer base.

Roadmap:
1. Market Analysis: Identify target industries, market demand for specialty chemicals, and competitive landscape analysis.
2. Product Development: Collaborate with clients to develop customized chemical solutions, conduct feasibility studies, and optimize formulations.
3. Manufacturing Setup: Establish manufacturing processes, quality assurance measures, and regulatory compliance frameworks.
4. Sales and Distribution: Develop sales strategies, build industry partnerships, and attend trade shows or exhibitions to showcase capabilities and secure contracts.

82. Customized Jewelry Design

Description: Launch a business specializing in customized jewelry design, offering bespoke pieces tailored to individual preferences and occasions, ranging from engagement rings to personalized accessories.

Marketing Insights and Opportunities:
- Personalization: Emphasize the ability to create unique, one-of-a-kind jewelry pieces that reflect personal stories, style preferences, and meaningful occasions.
- Gift Market: Target gift-giving occasions such as weddings, anniversaries, and holidays by promoting custom jewelry as sentimental and thoughtful gifts.

Requirements to Start:
- Design Expertise: Employ skilled jewelry designers capable of translating client ideas into intricate designs using CAD software and traditional techniques.
- Workshop Setup: Establish a jewelry workshop equipped with tools for metalworking, stone setting, and jewelry assembly.

Challenges:
- Client Expectations: Meet client expectations for design creativity, craftsmanship quality, and timely delivery within budget constraints.
- Material Sourcing: Source high-quality precious metals, gemstones, and other materials while managing costs and supplier relationships.

Scalability Opportunities:
- Online Presence: Develop an e-commerce platform showcasing portfolio, customization options, and client testimonials to reach a global audience.
- Collaborations: Partner with wedding planners, fashion boutiques, and luxury retailers to expand distribution channels and increase brand visibility.

Roadmap:
1. Portfolio Development: Build a diverse portfolio of custom jewelry designs, including rings, necklaces, bracelets, and earrings.
2. Client Acquisition: Implement marketing strategies such as social media campaigns, influencer partnerships, and participation in bridal shows or jewelry exhibitions.
3. Operational Efficiency: Streamline production processes, inventory management, and client communication to enhance customer experience and business scalability.
4. Brand Building: Cultivate brand identity through storytelling, customer engagement, and reputation management to differentiate from competitors and build brand loyalty.

Tourism and Hospitality Businesses

Starting a business in tourism and hospitality involves offering unique experiences and accommodations tailored to travelers' preferences, whether it's cultural tours, boutique hotels, or adventure travel.

83. Cultural Tours and Experiences

Description: Establish a business specializing in cultural tours and experiences, offering travelers immersive journeys into local traditions, history, arts, and cuisine of specific regions or countries.

Marketing Insights and Opportunities:
- Authentic Experiences: Highlight authentic encounters with local culture, guided tours to historical landmarks, cultural workshops, and culinary experiences.
- Target Audience: Appeal to culturally curious travelers seeking meaningful interactions and deeper insights into destination cultures.

Requirements to Start:
- Local Expertise. Recruit knowledgeable guides or cultural experts with insights into local customs, languages, and historical significance.
- Partnerships: Establish partnerships with local businesses, museums, cultural centers, and artisans to enhance tour offerings and authenticity.

Challenges:
- Seasonality: Manage seasonal fluctuations in tourist demand and optimize tour schedules and offerings accordingly.
- Logistics: Coordinate transportation, accommodation, and permits for group tours while ensuring smooth execution of cultural activities.

Scalability Opportunities:
- Diversified Offerings: Expand tour themes to include niche interests such as eco-tourism, heritage tours, culinary trails, and arts-focused experiences.
- Digital Presence: Develop a user-friendly website, leverage social media platforms, and collaborate with travel agencies to reach global travelers and travel enthusiasts.

Roadmap:
1. Destination Research: Identify target destinations, cultural attractions, and unique selling points to design compelling tour itineraries.
2. Service Development: Customize tour packages, pricing structures, and optional add-ons based on market research and customer feedback.
3. Marketing Strategy: Implement online and offline marketing campaigns, SEO strategies, and partnerships with travel influencers to increase visibility and bookings.
4. Customer Experience: Prioritize customer satisfaction through personalized service, safety measures, and post-tour feedback analysis for continuous improvement.

84. Boutique Hotel Chain

Description: Launch a chain of boutique hotels characterized by unique themes, personalized service, and distinctive architecture or interior design, catering to discerning travelers seeking intimate and upscale accommodations.

Marketing Insights and Opportunities:
- Unique Offerings: Showcase each hotel's distinct personality, amenities, and local charm to attract guests seeking authentic and memorable experiences.
- Target Demographics: Appeal to affluent travelers, business executives, and leisure seekers looking for luxury and exclusivity.

Requirements to Start:
- Property Acquisition: Identify and acquire suitable properties in desirable locations conducive to boutique hotel concepts.
- Interior Design: Collaborate with interior designers, architects, and local artisans to create captivating aesthetics and ambiance that reflect the hotel's theme.

Challenges:
- Operational Excellence: Maintain high standards of service, cleanliness, and hospitality to uphold the boutique hotel brand's reputation.
- Market Differentiation: Differentiate from chain hotels through personalized service, unique amenities, and curated guest experiences.

Scalability Opportunities:
- Brand Expansion: Expand the boutique hotel chain into new markets, both domestic and international, while maintaining consistency in quality and guest experience.
- Partnerships: Form strategic partnerships with travel agencies, event planners, and corporate clients to increase occupancy rates and revenue streams.

Roadmap:
1. Concept Development: Define the boutique hotel's theme, target market, and guest experience philosophy to guide property selection and design.
2. Property Renovation: Renovate or refurbish acquired properties to align with brand standards, emphasizing comfort, aesthetics, and sustainability.
3. Marketing and Branding: Develop a comprehensive branding strategy, website design, and digital marketing campaigns to build brand awareness and attract guests.
4. Guest Engagement: Implement guest loyalty programs, personalized concierge services, and feedback mechanisms to enhance guest satisfaction and loyalty.

85. Adventure Travel Agency

Description: Start an adventure travel agency specializing in organizing and coordinating adrenaline-pumping experiences such as hiking, mountaineering, safari tours, and extreme sports activities.

Marketing Insights and Opportunities:

- Adventure Seekers: Target adventure enthusiasts, thrill-seekers, and eco-tourists seeking unique and challenging outdoor experiences.
- Destination Diversity: Offer diverse adventure packages in remote wilderness areas, national parks, and off-the-beaten-path locations worldwide.

Requirements to Start:
- Destination Knowledge: Hire experienced guides and outdoor experts with knowledge of local terrain, safety protocols, and emergency response.
- Licensing and Permits: Obtain necessary licenses, permits, and insurance coverage for conducting adventure activities in different locations.

Challenges:
- Safety and Risk Management: Prioritize participant safety through thorough risk assessments, trained guides, and adherence to international safety standards.
- Seasonal Demand: Manage seasonal variations in weather conditions and tourist preferences for specific adventure activities.

Scalability Opportunities:
- Specialized Tours: Expand offerings to include niche adventure activities such as wildlife safaris, scuba diving expeditions, and cultural immersion experiences.
- Digital Presence: Enhance online visibility through SEO, social media marketing, and partnerships with travel influencers to attract global adventure travelers.

Roadmap:
1. Adventure Portfolio: Develop a portfolio of adventure packages, including detailed itineraries, activity schedules, and accommodation options.
2. Guide Training: Provide comprehensive training for guides in outdoor leadership, first aid, navigation, and customer service.
3. Marketing Strategy: Promote adventure tours through targeted digital marketing campaigns, adventure travel expos, and partnerships with travel agencies.
4. Customer Experience: Focus on personalized service, eco-friendly practices, and community engagement to foster positive reviews and repeat business.

86. Eco-Tourism Packages

Description: Develop eco-tourism packages that promote sustainable travel practices, wildlife conservation, and cultural immersion experiences in environmentally sensitive areas.

Marketing Insights and Opportunities:
- Sustainability Focus: Highlight eco-friendly accommodations, carbon-neutral travel options, and community-driven tourism initiatives.
- Educational Value: Appeal to environmentally conscious travelers seeking educational insights into local ecosystems, conservation efforts, and sustainable living practices.

Requirements to Start:

- Local Partnerships: Collaborate with conservation organizations, local communities, and eco-lodges to create authentic eco-tourism experiences.
- Expert Guides: Recruit knowledgeable guides with expertise in biodiversity, ecology, and local culture to lead eco-tours responsibly.

Challenges:
- Environmental Impact: Minimize ecological footprints through responsible tourism practices, waste management, and wildlife protection measures.
- Community Engagement: Address local community concerns, respect cultural sensitivities, and contribute positively to socio-economic development.

Scalability Opportunities:
- Destination Expansion: Expand eco-tourism offerings to new geographic regions, leveraging diverse ecosystems and cultural diversity.
- Educational Workshops: Offer eco-tourism workshops, volunteer programs, and immersive learning experiences to engage travelers and foster long-term sustainability practices.

Roadmap:
1. Destination Assessment: Conduct environmental assessments, stakeholder consultations, and feasibility studies to select eco-friendly travel destinations.
2. Package Development: Design eco-tourism itineraries featuring nature walks, wildlife safaris, bird watching tours, and sustainable agriculture visits.
3. Marketing Strategy: Implement digital marketing campaigns, eco-travel blogs, and partnerships with eco-conscious travel agencies to promote eco-tourism packages.
4. Guest Experience: Focus on personalized service, eco-certified accommodations, and interactive activities to enhance guest satisfaction and loyalty.

87. Local Food and Farm Tours

Description: Establish a business offering guided tours that showcase local culinary delights, farms, dairy farms, and farm-to-table dining experiences in diverse gastronomic regions.

Marketing Insights and Opportunities:
- Culinary Experiences: Highlight gourmet tastings, cooking classes, and food pairings that celebrate regional cuisine and artisanal products.
- Farm and Dairy Tourism: Attract families enthusiasts with farm tours, straight from farm tastings, dairy visits, and exclusive farm events hosted by local farmers.

Requirements to Start:
- Local Partnerships: Forge relationships with restaurants, farms, farmers' markets, and culinary artisans to curate authentic food experiences.
- Certified Guides: Employ certified tour guides with expertise in local cuisine, food culture and dairy production methods.

Challenges:

- Logistical Coordination: Coordinate transportation, reservations, and itinerary planning to ensure seamless guest experiences and logistical efficiency.
- Seasonal Variability: Navigate seasonal fluctuations in crop harvests, restaurant availability, and tourist demand for food and dairy tours.

Scalability Opportunities:
- Customized Tours: Develop themed tours based on seasonal harvests, food festivals, cultural celebrations, and culinary trends to attract diverse clientele.
- Digital Marketing: Enhance online presence through farm and dairy tourism websites, social media platforms, and partnerships with travel agencies and gourmet clubs.

Roadmap:
1. Destination Selection: Identify culinary hotspots, dairy regions, and gastronomic capitals known for their local food specialties and dairy production.
2. Experience Development: Create curated farm and dairy tour packages, including tasting menus, chef-led workshops, and behind-the-scenes culinary experiences.
3. Promotion Strategy: Launch targeted marketing campaigns, culinary blogs, and partnerships with food influencers to attract food enthusiasts.
4. Customer Engagement: Collect guest feedback, offer loyalty programs, and cultivate relationships with local suppliers and hospitality providers to enhance guest satisfaction.

88. Luxury Yacht Charter Services

Description: Launch a luxury yacht charter business offering bespoke sailing experiences, private cruises, and yacht rentals for affluent travelers seeking exclusive maritime adventures.

Marketing Insights and Opportunities:
- Exclusivity: Emphasize personalized itineraries, gourmet dining, onboard amenities, and VIP services tailored to luxury yacht charter clients.
- Destination Focus: Promote yacht charters in exotic locations, coastal paradises, and sailing hotspots renowned for scenic beauty and nautical adventures.

Requirements to Start:
- Yacht Fleet Acquisition: Acquire or lease luxury yachts equipped with state-of-the-art navigation systems, luxury accommodations, and recreational facilities.
- Crew Expertise: Recruit skilled captains, crew members, and hospitality staff trained in maritime safety, guest services, and yacht maintenance.

Challenges:
- Regulatory Compliance: Adhere to maritime laws, safety regulations, and environmental standards governing yacht operations and passenger safety.
- Seasonal Demand: Manage peak seasons, booking schedules, and logistical challenges associated with yacht availability and charter reservations.

Scalability Opportunities:

- Fleet Expansion: Expand yacht fleet size, diversity, and luxury offerings to accommodate varying client preferences and group sizes.
- Destination Diversification: Introduce yacht charters in new sailing destinations, collaborate with luxury resorts, and offer integrated travel packages for seamless guest experiences.

Roadmap:
1. Yacht Selection: Curate a portfolio of luxury yachts, catamarans, and sailboats catering to different client preferences, from family vacations to corporate retreats.
2. Service Differentiation: Design bespoke itineraries, onboard activities, and themed events tailored to luxury yacht charter clients' preferences and special occasions.
3. Marketing Strategy: Establish a strong online presence, luxury travel partnerships, and yacht charter directories to attract high-net-worth individuals and yacht enthusiasts.
4. Client Relations: Provide personalized concierge services, yacht maintenance updates, and 24/7 customer support to ensure exceptional guest experiences and client satisfaction.

Social Impact and Nonprofit Businesses

Starting a business with a social impact or nonprofit focus involves addressing community needs, promoting social welfare, and enhancing quality of life through innovative solutions and programs.

89. Community Kitchen and Food Distribution

Description: Establish a community kitchen and food distribution initiative aimed at providing nutritious meals, food security, and culinary education to underserved populations.

Marketing Insights and Opportunities:
- Community Engagement: Foster community partnerships, volunteer involvement, and donations to support sustainable food distribution and meal programs.
- Nutritional Education: Offer cooking classes, nutrition workshops, and food literacy programs to empower individuals and families with culinary skills and healthy eating habits.

Requirements to Start:
- Kitchen Infrastructure: Equip a commercial kitchen with cooking appliances, food storage facilities, and sanitation standards compliant with health regulations.
- Partnerships: Collaborate with local farms, food banks, restaurants, and volunteers to source ingredients, prepare meals, and distribute food to beneficiaries.

Challenges:
- Sustainability: Secure ongoing funding, donations, and community support to sustain food operations, kitchen maintenance, and meal delivery logistics.
- Logistics Management: Coordinate food procurement, meal preparation, and distribution schedules to ensure timely and equitable access to nutritious meals.

Scalability Opportunities:
- Expansion: Scale kitchen operations to serve more communities, establish satellite kitchens, and collaborate with government agencies and corporate sponsors to expand food distribution networks.
- Educational Outreach: Develop partnerships with schools, healthcare providers, and community centers to promote food security, healthy eating habits, and culinary education initiatives.

Roadmap:
1. Needs Assessment: Conduct community needs assessments, food insecurity surveys, and stakeholder consultations to identify target populations and food distribution priorities.
2. Kitchen Setup: Acquire kitchen equipment, storage facilities, and food handling certifications required for safe food preparation and storage.

3. Program Development: Design meal programs, nutritional guidelines, and volunteer training protocols to ensure quality food services and community engagement.
4. Fundraising and Awareness: Launch fundraising campaigns, community events, and social media campaigns to raise awareness, solicit donations, and recruit volunteers for sustainable food initiatives.

Further Resources:
- World Food Programme

90. Mobile Health Clinics

Description: Launch mobile health clinics to provide accessible healthcare services, preventive care, and medical screenings to underserved communities and vulnerable populations.

Marketing Insights and Opportunities:
- Health Equity: Address healthcare disparities by offering mobile clinics in rural areas, urban neighborhoods, and underserved regions lacking access to medical facilities.
- Partnership Collaboration: Partner with healthcare providers, nonprofit organizations, and local governments to expand healthcare access and promote community wellness.

Requirements to Start:
- Mobile Unit Setup: Equip mobile clinics with medical equipment, diagnostic tools, and telehealth capabilities to deliver primary care, vaccinations, and chronic disease management services.
- Licensed Healthcare Providers: Recruit licensed physicians, nurses, and healthcare professionals to staff mobile clinics and provide comprehensive medical care.

Challenges:
- Regulatory Compliance: Navigate licensing, insurance, and regulatory requirements for operating mobile healthcare facilities and delivering telemedicine services.
- Resource Allocation: Secure funding, grants, and community support to sustain mobile clinic operations, medical supplies, and staff salaries.

Scalability Opportunities:
- Health Education: Expand services to include health education workshops, preventive screenings, and wellness programs tailored to diverse community health needs.
- Partnership Expansion: Forge partnerships with universities, corporate sponsors, and healthcare technology providers to enhance mobile clinic capabilities and reach more underserved populations.

Roadmap:
1. Needs Assessment: Conduct community health assessments, demographic studies, and healthcare utilization analyses to identify priority health issues and target service areas.

2. Mobile Clinic Design: Customize mobile units with patient exam rooms, telemedicine stations, pharmacy services, and wheelchair accessibility to accommodate diverse patient needs.
3. Program Implementation: Develop healthcare protocols, patient registration systems, and electronic health record (EHR) integration for seamless care coordination and patient follow-up.
4. Community Engagement: Organize health fairs, outreach events, and mobile clinic tours to raise awareness, build trust, and promote healthcare access in underserved communities.

91. Youth Mentorship Program

Description: Launch a youth mentorship program offering guidance, academic support, career readiness, and personal development opportunities for at-risk youth and adolescents.

Marketing Insights and Opportunities:
- Empowerment Focus: Empower youth through mentorship, leadership development, and skill-building workshops to foster academic success and career aspirations.
- Community Collaboration: Collaborate with schools, youth organizations, and local businesses to create mentorship networks and internship opportunities for program participants.

Requirements to Start:
- Mentor Recruitment: Recruit volunteer mentors, professionals, and role models from diverse backgrounds to mentor youth and provide guidance on educational and career pathways.
- Program Curriculum: Develop curriculum modules, workshops, and mentoring activities tailored to age-specific needs, academic goals, and personal growth objectives.

Challenges:
- Retention and Engagement: Maintain long-term mentor-mentee relationships, track program outcomes, and measure impact on academic achievement, career readiness, and personal development.
- Resource Mobilization: Secure funding, grants, and corporate sponsorships to sustain mentorship program operations, recruit mentors, and provide youth enrichment activities.

Scalability Opportunities:
- Expansion: Expand mentorship program initiatives to serve more youth populations, partner with schools, community centers, and juvenile justice programs to reach at-risk youth.
- Skill Development: Offer vocational training, internship placements, and entrepreneurial workshops to empower youth with practical skills and professional experiences.

Roadmap:

1. Community Needs Assessment: Identify youth demographics, educational challenges, and socio-economic barriers to determine mentorship program priorities and target populations.
2. Mentor Training: Provide mentor orientation, training workshops, and ongoing support to equip mentors with effective communication, leadership, and mentoring skills.
3. Program Evaluation: Implement evaluation metrics, participant surveys, and impact assessments to measure mentorship program effectiveness and youth outcomes.
4. Partnership Development: Collaborate with schools, youth agencies, corporate sponsors, and local stakeholders to build strategic alliances, secure funding, and expand program resources.

92. Environmental Conservation Nonprofit

Description: Establish an environmental conservation nonprofit organization dedicated to preserving natural habitats, promoting sustainable practices, and raising awareness about environmental issues.

Marketing Insights and Opportunities:
- Environmental Advocacy: Advocate for environmental stewardship, conservation initiatives, and eco-friendly practices through education, community outreach, and policy advocacy.
- Collaborative Partnerships: Form alliances with environmental agencies, conservation groups, and corporate sponsors to fund projects, organize events, and implement conservation programs.

Requirements to Start:
- Project Funding: Secure grants, donations, and sponsorships to support environmental projects, habitat restoration efforts, and wildlife conservation programs.
- Volunteer Engagement: Recruit volunteers, conservationists, and environmental scientists to participate in fieldwork, research projects, and community clean-up events.

Challenges:
- Sustainability: Ensure long-term funding sustainability, volunteer retention, and public support for ongoing environmental conservation efforts and outreach programs.
- Regulatory Compliance: Navigate environmental laws, permits, and regulations governing conservation activities, habitat restoration projects, and wildlife protection measures.

Scalability Opportunities:
- Expansion Projects: Expand conservation initiatives to new regions, biodiversity hotspots, and critical ecosystems threatened by habitat loss, climate change, and environmental degradation.
- Education and Outreach: Develop educational programs, eco-tours, and environmental workshops to engage schools, universities, and local communities in conservation awareness and action.

Roadmap:
1. Environmental Assessment: Conduct habitat surveys, biodiversity assessments, and ecological research to identify priority conservation areas and species protection strategies.
2. Program Development: Design conservation projects, habitat restoration plans, and sustainable resource management initiatives aligned with environmental conservation goals and community needs.
3. Public Awareness: Launch awareness campaigns, environmental forums, and eco-events to mobilize public support, inspire environmental activism, and promote eco-friendly lifestyles.
4. Collaborative Impact: Forge partnerships with government agencies, conservation NGOs, and corporate sponsors to leverage resources, expertise, and collective efforts for greater conservation impact.

Further Resources:
- World Wildlife Fund (WWF)

93. Refugee Support Services

Description: Establish refugee support services offering resettlement assistance, humanitarian aid, and integration programs to help refugees rebuild their lives in host communities.

Marketing Insights and Opportunities:
- Humanitarian Aid: Provide emergency relief, shelter assistance, and basic necessities to refugees displaced by conflict, persecution, and humanitarian crises.
- Integration Support: Offer language classes, cultural orientation workshops, and job placement services to facilitate refugee integration, socio-economic empowerment, and community cohesion.

Requirements to Start:
- Partnership Building: Collaborate with refugee agencies, humanitarian organizations, and local governments to coordinate refugee resettlement efforts, legal advocacy, and social services.
- Volunteer Recruitment: Recruit volunteers, interpreters, and cultural liaisons to support refugee families, offer emotional support, and assist with daily living activities.

Challenges:
- Resource Mobilization: Secure funding, donations, and in-kind contributions to sustain refugee assistance programs, housing subsidies, and educational opportunities for refugee youth.
- Cultural Sensitivity: Address cultural differences, language barriers, and trauma-informed care to provide culturally competent services and support to diverse refugee populations.

Scalability Opportunities:

- Program Expansion: Expand refugee support services to new geographic areas, refugee camps, and host communities experiencing refugee influxes and displacement crises.
- Advocacy and Awareness: Advocate for refugee rights, immigration policies, and humanitarian assistance through public campaigns, advocacy forums, and community partnerships.

Roadmap:
1. Needs Assessment: Assess refugee needs, demographic profiles, and resettlement challenges to tailor support services, advocacy initiatives, and community outreach strategies.
2. Service Coordination: Establish case management systems, referral networks, and partnership agreements to ensure coordinated service delivery and holistic support for refugee families.
3. Community Engagement: Organize cultural events, intercultural dialogue sessions, and volunteer opportunities to promote refugee integration, mutual understanding, and social cohesion.
4. Policy Advocacy: Collaborate with policymakers, human rights organizations, and refugee advocacy groups to influence immigration policies, asylum procedures, and refugee protection laws.

Further Resources:
- UN Refugee Agency (UNHCR)

94. Animal Rescue and Adoption Center

Description: Establish an animal rescue and adoption center dedicated to rescuing, rehabilitating, and rooming abandoned, abused, and neglected animals.

Marketing Insights and Opportunities:
- Animal Welfare Advocacy: Promote responsible pet ownership, animal rights, and humane treatment through adoption events, education campaigns, and community outreach.
- Collaborative Partnerships: Partner with veterinary clinics, animal shelters, and pet supply stores to facilitate pet adoptions, foster care programs, and veterinary care services.

Requirements to Start:
- Facility Setup: Secure a facility with kennels, animal habitats, veterinary equipment, and sanitation protocols compliant with animal welfare standards and regulations.
- Animal Care Expertise: Recruit veterinarians, animal behaviorists, and trained staff to provide medical care, behavioral assessments, and enrichment activities for rescued animals.

Challenges:
- Funding Constraints: Secure funding through donations, adoption fees, and fundraising events to cover operating costs, veterinary expenses, and animal care supplies.

- Animal Overpopulation: Address pet overpopulation challenges through spay/neuter programs, public education campaigns, and community outreach initiatives promoting responsible pet ownership.

Scalability Opportunities:
- Community Outreach: Expand adoption outreach programs, humane education initiatives, and volunteer opportunities to engage schools, youth groups, and corporate sponsors in animal welfare advocacy.
- Collaborative Partnerships: Foster partnerships with rescue networks, animal welfare organizations, and pet-related businesses to facilitate pet transports, cross-promotional events, and animal care workshops.

Roadmap:
1. Rescue Operations: Develop rescue protocols, intake procedures, and medical evaluation standards to assess and prioritize animal rescue cases based on health status, behavioral needs, and rehabilitation potential.
2. Adoption Programs: Implement adoption screenings, foster care programs, and adoption counseling services to match rescued animals with suitable adoptive families and promote lifelong pet welfare.
3. Community Engagement: Organize adoption events, fundraising campaigns, and volunteer orientations to build community support, raise awareness about animal welfare issues, and recruit dedicated animal advocates.
4. Advocacy Efforts: Advocate for animal protection laws, anti-cruelty legislation, and animal welfare policies through public advocacy campaigns, legislative lobbying, and coalition-building efforts with animal rights organizations.

Miscellaneous Business Ideas

95. Pet Care and Grooming Services

Description: Provide professional pet grooming services, including bathing, hair trimming, and nail clipping, along with pet care options such as boarding and daycare.

Marketing Insights and Opportunities:
- Pet Owners' Needs: Address the growing demand for convenient and reliable pet grooming services that prioritize animal welfare and customer satisfaction.
- Specialized Services: Offer add-on services like dental care, flea treatments, and spa treatments to enhance the grooming experience and meet pet owners' expectations.

Requirements to Start:
- Grooming Facility: Establish a well-equipped grooming salon with grooming tables, tubs, grooming tools, and pet-safe products for bathing and grooming procedures.
- Certified Groomers: Hire certified groomers with experience in handling different pet breeds, grooming techniques, and animal behavior to ensure quality care and safety.

Challenges:
- Competitive Market: Navigate competition from local groomers, pet spas, and mobile grooming services by offering superior customer service, competitive pricing, and specialized grooming packages.
- Pet Safety: Maintain high standards of hygiene, sanitation, and pet handling practices to prevent injuries, infections, and ensure the well-being of all animals under care.

Scalability Opportunities:
- Expansion Services: Expand services to include mobile grooming options, pet pickup/drop-off services, and pet grooming workshops for pet owners interested in DIY grooming techniques.
- Franchise Model: Explore franchising opportunities to replicate the business model in new markets, collaborate with pet-related businesses, and extend brand presence nationally or internationally.

Roadmap:
1. Market Research: Conduct market research, competitor analysis, and customer surveys to identify local pet grooming preferences, service gaps, and potential target demographics.
2. Business Setup: Secure permits, licenses, and insurance coverage required for operating a pet grooming business, adhere to health and safety regulations, and invest in grooming equipment and facility improvements.
3. Service Development: Develop grooming service menus, pricing structures, and promotional packages tailored to pet owners' preferences, seasonal demands, and special occasions.
4. Marketing Strategy: Implement digital marketing campaigns, social media promotions, and community outreach events to build brand awareness, attract new clients, and foster customer loyalty through positive reviews and referrals.

96. Subscription Service for Seniors

Description: Launch a subscription service offering curated products, essentials, or activities tailored to the needs and interests of senior citizens.

Marketing Insights and Opportunities:
- Senior Market Demand: Address the growing market for subscription services catering to seniors' convenience, independence, and personalized lifestyle preferences.
- Health and Wellness: Offer subscription boxes with health products, mobility aids, educational materials, and leisure activities to enhance seniors' quality of life and social engagement.

Requirements to Start:
- Subscription Model: Develop subscription plans, product offerings, and pricing tiers based on seniors' preferences, budget considerations, and subscription box customization options.
- Supplier Partnerships: Establish partnerships with suppliers, manufacturers, and vendors to source high-quality products, durable goods, and specialized items suitable for seniors.

Challenges:
- Customer Acquisition: Build trust, educate seniors and caregivers about subscription benefits, and address concerns about product quality, affordability, and subscription flexibility.
- Logistics Management: Manage inventory, order fulfillment, and subscription box customization to meet seniors' unique needs, dietary restrictions, and lifestyle preferences effectively.

Scalability Opportunities:
- Personalization Options: Expand subscription offerings to include personalized care packages, seasonal themes, and gift subscriptions for family members seeking thoughtful, practical gifts for seniors.
- Community Engagement: Partner with senior centers, retirement communities, and healthcare providers to promote subscription services, offer trial subscriptions, and host informational sessions on aging-in-place solutions.

Roadmap:
1. Market Analysis: Conduct demographic research, senior consumer behavior analysis, and competitor benchmarking to identify niche subscription opportunities, service differentiators, and growth potential.
2. Product Curation: Curate subscription box themes, product selections, and add-on options that resonate with seniors' lifestyle preferences, hobbies, and daily living needs.
3. Subscription Management: Implement user-friendly subscription management software, customer service protocols, and subscription renewal strategies to optimize user experience, retention rates, and customer satisfaction.

4. Marketing and Outreach: Launch targeted marketing campaigns, digital advertising initiatives, and social media promotions to reach seniors, caregivers, and family members interested in subscription services that enhance seniors' well-being, convenience, and social connectivity.

97. Event Planning and Coordination

Description: Provide comprehensive event planning and coordination services for corporate events, weddings, parties, and special occasions.

Marketing Insights and Opportunities:
- Event Industry Demand: Capitalize on the demand for professional event planners, venue coordination, and personalized event experiences that exceed client expectations.
- Specialized Services: Offer event styling, theme development, catering services, and entertainment options to create memorable, seamless event experiences for clients and guests.

Requirements to Start:
- Event Planning Expertise: Employ experienced event planners, coordinators, and event staff with expertise in logistics management, vendor negotiations, and client relations to ensure event success.
- Vendor Partnerships: Establish partnerships with venues, caterers, decorators, and entertainment providers to offer diverse event services, customized packages, and competitive pricing options.

Challenges:
- Competitive Market: Navigate competition from established event planning firms, freelance planners, and DIY event organizers by offering unique event concepts, personalized service, and professional event management expertise.
- Client Expectations: Manage client expectations, budget constraints, and last-minute changes while maintaining service quality, event timelines, and seamless guest experiences.

Scalability Opportunities:
- Event Portfolio Expansion: Expand service offerings to include destination weddings, corporate retreats, virtual events, and hybrid event solutions that cater to diverse client preferences and event planning needs.
- Industry Networking: Network with industry professionals, hospitality partners, and event vendors to access new markets, referral opportunities, and collaborative event projects that enhance business growth and reputation.

Roadmap:
1. Market Research: Conduct market research, client surveys, and industry trend analysis to identify event planning trends, client preferences, and market opportunities for specialized event services.

2. Business Development: Develop event planning packages, service agreements, and event proposal templates that outline service offerings, pricing structures, and customization options tailored to client needs.
3. Project Management: Implement event planning software, project management tools, and event logistics checklists to streamline event coordination, vendor communications, and client updates throughout the event planning process.
4. Marketing Strategy: Launch targeted marketing campaigns, social media promotions, and networking events to build brand awareness, attract new clients, and cultivate long-term partnerships with corporate clients, wedding planners, and event industry professionals.

98. Car Rental and Ride-Sharing Service

Description: Launch a hybrid car rental and ride-sharing service offering flexible rental options and on-demand transportation solutions.

Marketing Insights and Opportunities:
- Urban Mobility: Address urban commuters' need for convenient, cost-effective transportation options with flexible rental terms, ride-sharing features, and competitive pricing.
- Travel Convenience: Provide airport pickup/drop-off services, long-term rentals, and vehicle customization options to cater to travelers, tourists, and business professionals.

Requirements to Start:
- Fleet Acquisition: Acquire a diverse fleet of vehicles, including economy cars, luxury vehicles, and eco-friendly options, equipped with GPS tracking, safety features, and maintenance records.
- Insurance and Licensing: Obtain commercial insurance coverage, vehicle permits, and licensing requirements to operate a car rental and ride-sharing service legally and responsibly.

Challenges:
- Regulatory Compliance: Navigate local transportation regulations, licensing requirements, and safety standards governing vehicle operation, driver qualifications, and passenger safety.
- Customer Trust: Build customer trust, reliability, and brand reputation through transparent pricing, responsive customer service, and driver background checks for enhanced security.

Scalability Opportunities:
- Market Expansion: Expand service coverage to new cities, tourist destinations, and transportation hubs to increase market reach, customer base, and business growth opportunities.
- Technology Integration: Implement mobile app features, real-time booking systems, and digital payment solutions to streamline vehicle reservations, ride-sharing requests, and customer feedback.

Roadmap:
1. Market Analysis: Conduct market research, competitor analysis, and customer surveys to identify local transportation needs, market gaps, and potential demand for car rental and ride-sharing services.
2. Business Setup: Establish strategic partnerships with car manufacturers, leasing companies, and transportation networks to optimize fleet management, vehicle maintenance, and operational efficiency.
3. Customer Acquisition: Launch promotional campaigns, referral programs, and loyalty rewards to attract new customers, retain loyal clients, and build long-term relationships through exceptional service delivery.
4. Expansion Strategy: Explore franchise opportunities, partnership agreements, and collaborative ventures with hospitality providers, travel agencies, and corporate clients to expand service offerings, increase revenue streams, and achieve sustainable business growth.

Further Resources:
- Uber

99. Language Translation Services

Description: Establish a language translation agency offering professional translation, localization, and interpretation services for businesses, organizations, and individuals.

Marketing Insights and Opportunities:
- Globalization Trends: Capitalize on globalization, international business expansion, and multicultural communication needs with accurate, culturally sensitive translation services.
- Sector Specialization: Offer industry-specific translations, technical documentation, and legal interpretation services tailored to client requirements, regulatory standards, and target audience preferences.

Requirements to Start:
- Translator Network: Build a team of certified translators, bilingual professionals, and subject matter experts proficient in diverse languages, dialects, and specialized fields.
- Translation Tools: Invest in translation software, CAT tools (Computer-Assisted Translation), and linguistic resources to ensure translation accuracy, consistency, and workflow efficiency.

Challenges:
- Quality Assurance: Maintain translation quality, linguistic accuracy, and cultural relevance through rigorous proofreading, editing, and client feedback processes to meet client expectations and industry standards.
- Confidentiality: Ensure data privacy, client confidentiality, and secure file handling practices when managing sensitive documents, legal contracts, and proprietary information for translation projects.

Scalability Opportunities:

- Language Expertise: Expand language offerings, interpreter services, and multilingual support to serve diverse client needs, international markets, and language-specific localization projects.
- Technology Integration: Adopt AI-driven translation solutions, machine learning algorithms, and automated workflows to optimize translation processes, reduce turnaround times, and enhance service scalability.

Roadmap:
1. Market Research: Conduct market analysis, competitor benchmarking, and client surveys to identify language service trends, customer preferences, and industry-specific translation demands.
2. Service Portfolio: Develop service packages, pricing models, and service level agreements (SLAs) for document translation, website localization, multimedia content, and simultaneous interpretation services.
3. Client Acquisition: Implement digital marketing strategies, SEO optimization, and content localization to attract global clients, enhance online visibility, and generate leads through targeted marketing campaigns.
4. Quality Control: Establish quality assurance protocols, translation memory databases, and terminological glossaries to ensure consistency, accuracy, and adherence to industry standards across all translation projects.

100. Vintage Car Restoration

Description: Launch a vintage car restoration service specializing in restoring classic automobiles to their original condition or customized specifications.

Marketing Insights and Opportunities:
- Classic Car Enthusiasts: Tap into the niche market of vintage car collectors, enthusiasts, and automotive museums seeking expert restoration craftsmanship, historical accuracy, and vehicle preservation.
- Customization Trends: Offer custom restoration services, performance upgrades, and personalized design modifications to enhance vintage car aesthetics, functionality, and market value.

Requirements to Start:
- Workshop Setup: Establish a fully equipped restoration workshop with specialized tools, equipment, and restoration facilities capable of handling classic car refurbishment, bodywork repairs, and mechanical overhauls.
- Expertise and Talent: Recruit skilled automotive craftsmen, restoration specialists, and vintage car mechanics with experience in classic car restoration techniques, craftsmanship, and historical preservation.

Challenges:
- Authenticity: Preserve vehicle authenticity, historical accuracy, and original components while conducting restoration work, part replacements, and customization upgrades to meet client specifications and industry standards.

- Cost Management: Manage restoration costs, project timelines, and client budget expectations through transparent pricing, detailed project estimates, and phased restoration plans for complex restoration projects.

Scalability Opportunities:
- Specialized Services: Expand restoration services to include rare car models, exotic imports, and specialty vehicles with unique restoration challenges, technical requirements, and customization opportunities.
- Market Expansion: Collaborate with vintage car dealerships, auction houses, and automotive restoration networks to access new markets, client referrals, and restoration projects on a national or international scale.

Roadmap:
1. Client Consultation: Conduct initial vehicle assessments, restoration consultations, and project feasibility studies to outline restoration goals, client expectations, and restoration milestones.
2. Restoration Process: Develop restoration plans, repair schedules, and restoration techniques tailored to vehicle condition, restoration scope, and client preferences for vintage car preservation and enhancement.
3. Quality Assurance: Implement quality control measures, restoration benchmarks, and post-restoration inspections to ensure craftsmanship, vehicle performance, and client satisfaction with restored classic cars.
4. Marketing Strategy: Showcase restoration portfolio, client testimonials, and restoration success stories through digital marketing campaigns, social media platforms, and automotive industry publications to attract vintage car enthusiasts, collectors, and restoration connoisseurs.

Conclusion

Congratulations on exploring these 100 diverse business ideas spanning various sectors and industries. Each idea has been meticulously crafted to inspire and guide you towards entrepreneurial success. Whether you're a seasoned entrepreneur looking for your next venture or someone just starting out, these ideas intend to spark creativity, innovation, and strategic thinking.

Throughout this book, we've delved into a wide array of business opportunities, from technology and innovation to retail, services, consulting, and beyond. Each idea was meant to be presented with detailed insights into market opportunities, challenges, scalability potential, and practical steps to get started.

I believe the key to success lies not only in the idea itself but in your ability to execute it with passion, dedication, and a thorough understanding of your target market. Whether you choose to pursue a tech startup, launch an ecommerce venture, provide consulting services, or embark on a creative endeavor, the principles of entrepreneurship remain constant: identifying a need, providing value, and adapting to change.

Next Steps

1. Evaluate and Refine: Review the business ideas presented and consider which align best with your skills, interests, and market trends. Conduct further research and validation to refine your chosen idea.

2. Create a Business Plan: Develop a comprehensive business plan that outlines your business concept, target market, competitive analysis, marketing strategy, financial projections, and operational plan.

3. Build Your Network: Connect with industry professionals, mentors, potential customers, and suppliers within your chosen field. Networking can provide invaluable support, advice, and opportunities for collaboration.

4. Seek Funding: Explore funding options such as bootstrapping, loans, grants, or seeking investment from angel investors or venture capitalists, depending on your business needs and growth plans.

5. Execute with Passion: Launch your business with enthusiasm, dedication, and a commitment to delivering exceptional value to your customers. Stay adaptable and responsive to market feedback and evolving trends.

Final Thoughts

As you embark on your entrepreneurial journey, remember that entrepreneurship is a marathon, not a sprint. Embrace the challenges as opportunities for growth, learn from setbacks, and celebrate milestones along the way. Your journey will be unique, shaped by your vision, perseverance, and ability to innovate.

Stay true to your values, maintain integrity in your business dealings, and prioritize customer satisfaction. Keep learning, stay curious, and be open to evolving your business model as you navigate the dynamic landscape of entrepreneurship.

Above all, enjoy the process of building something meaningful and impactful. Whether your goal is financial independence, societal contribution, or personal fulfillment, the entrepreneurial path offers limitless possibilities for creativity, innovation, and making a difference in the world.

I hope this conclusion and final thoughts section encapsulates the essence of your book and inspire your readers to take actionable steps towards their entrepreneurial dreams.

Next Steps

1. Evaluate and Refine:
   - Identify Your Passion and Skills: Reflect on your interests, strengths, and expertise to choose a business idea that aligns with your passion.
     - Market Research: Conduct thorough market research to assess demand, competition, and potential profitability of your chosen business idea.
   - Validate Your Idea: Gather feedback from potential customers, industry experts, and advisors to validate market need and refine your business concept accordingly.

2. Create a Business Plan:

A business plan serves as a roadmap for your venture, outlining your business goals, strategies, and operational details. Here's a step-by-step guide to create a comprehensive business plan:

- **Executive Summary**: Summarize your business idea, goals, target market, competitive advantage, and financial projections. This section should provide a brief overview of your entire business plan.

- **Business Description**:
  - Mission Statement: Define the purpose and mission of your business.
  - Vision Statement: Outline your long-term goals and aspirations for the business.

- **Market Analysis**:
  - Industry Overview: Describe the industry landscape, trends, and growth prospects.
  - Target Market: Define your ideal customer demographics, behaviors, needs, and preferences.
  - Competitive Analysis: Identify key competitors, their strengths, weaknesses, and market positioning. Assess how your business will differentiate itself.

- **Organization and Management**:
  - Legal Structure: Specify your business structure (e.g., sole proprietorship, partnership, LLC, corporation).
  - Management Team: Introduce key team members, their roles, responsibilities, and relevant experience.

- **Product or Service Offering**:
  - Description: Provide a detailed description of your products or services, including features, benefits, and unique selling points.
  - Development Stage: Outline current development stage and future plans for product/service enhancements.

- **Marketing and Sales Strategy**:
  - Target Market Strategy: Detail how you will reach and attract your target market.
  - Marketing Plan: Describe your marketing tactics, channels (e.g., digital marketing, social media, content marketing), and promotional strategies.
  - Sales Strategy: Outline your sales approach, pricing strategy, distribution channels, and sales forecast.

- **Operations Plan**:
  - Production/Service Delivery: Explain how your products/services will be produced or delivered.
  - Location and Facilities: Describe your physical location, facilities, and operational setup requirements.
  - Technology: Outline the technology infrastructure needed to support operations (e.g., software, hardware).

- **Financial Plan**:
  - Startup Costs and Funding Requirements: Estimate initial startup costs and funding needed to launch your business.

- Revenue Projections: Forecast your sales revenue based on market analysis, pricing strategy, and sales forecasts.
- Expense Projections: Estimate ongoing operational expenses, including personnel, rent, utilities, marketing, and administrative costs.
- Financial Statements: Include projected income statement, cash flow statement, and balance sheet for the first few years of operation.

- Appendices:
- Supporting Documents: Include any additional documents such as resumes of key team members, legal agreements, market research data, and references.

3. Build Your Network:
- Industry Connections: Attend industry events, networking functions, and join professional associations to build relationships with potential partners, suppliers, and mentors.
- Advisory Board: Consider forming an advisory board or seeking mentorship from experienced entrepreneurs or industry experts who can provide guidance and advice.

4. Seek Funding:
- Types of Funding: Explore different funding options such as personal savings, loans, grants, angel investors, venture capital, crowdfunding, or government programs.
- Pitch Deck: Develop a compelling pitch deck summarizing your business plan and investment opportunity to present to potential investors or lenders.

5. Execute with Passion:
- Launch Strategy: Develop a launch plan outlining the steps and timeline for bringing your business to market.
- Monitor and Adapt: Continuously monitor market trends, customer feedback, and financial performance to make informed decisions and adapt your strategies as needed.